so strikingly on the Senate floor ~~~~~~~~~~~~~~~~~~~~ had
made him the greatest L in the Senate (had;) ~~~~~~~ is
was a ~~

~~the ability~~ not only to recognize the crucial moment
but to seize the moment — to strike, to act.

He had a will for decision + a gift for decision —
a will to ~~decide~~ decide, a will to act.

⌐For 3 years he had been ~~given~~ allowed to make very few decisions
of any real consequence.

⌐now, w O'D's words, he had to make a lot —
+ to make them fast. ~~+ to make them ✗~~

⌐and he made them ⊗ ~~~~~~~~~~~~~~

# # #

⌐The first was about when + how to leave the hospital.
S- Emory Roberts + Youngblood — had urged him to leave. #
↑

A moment later, another.
Kilduff. No wait

They rush to the car, ~~~~~~~~~~~~~~~~~

sits on the left   Johnson told him to get in the back seat
so that J was protected on two to side

Busby saw it in a glance. "He was ~~✗~~ in had
charge" B said. "~~~~~~~ ~~~~~~~" command."

+ into the plane

The word — + the thought —
of "Conspiracy" was in the air

It wasn't merely the P who had been shot; the Governor
had been shot, too! Had ~~+ the shot that had~~ he been a
target, too.

+ would J himself have been shot if had Yblood not
flung him to cover   so quickly ?

Working

ROBERT A. CARO

Working

Researching, Interviewing, Writing

ALFRED A. KNOPF   New York
2019

Knopf, Borzoi Books, and the colophon are registered trademarks of Penguin Random House LLC.

"The City-Shaper" originally appeared in *The New Yorker,* January 5, 1998.

Parts of "'Turn Every Page,'" "LBJA," "'Why Can't You Do a Biography of Napoleon?,'" "Tricks of the Trade," and "Interviewing Lady Bird Johnson" were excerpted in the January 28, 2019, issue of *The New Yorker.*

Grateful acknowledgment is made to the following for permission to reprint previously published material:

Harper's Magazine: "Carbon Footprint," an interview with Robert A. Caro and John R. MacArthur. Copyright © 2014 by *Harper's Magazine.* All rights reserved. Reprinted from the December 2014 issue by permission of *Harper's Magazine.*

The New York Times: "Sanctum Sanctorum for Writers" by Robert Caro, originally appeared in *The New York Times* on May 19, 1995. Copyright © 1995 by *The New York Times.* Reprinted by permission of *The New York Times.*

The Paris Review: Excerpts from "Robert Caro, The Art of Biography No. 5," an interview with Robert Caro and James Santel, originally appeared in *The Paris Review* (Issue 216, Spring 2016). Reprinted by permission of *The Paris Review.*

Library of Congress Cataloging-in-Publication Data
Names: Caro, Robert A., author.
Title: Working : researching, interviewing, writing / by Robert A. Caro.
Description: First edition. | New York : Alfred A. Knopf, 2019. | "This is a Borzoi book published by Alfred A. Knopf."
Identifiers: LCCN 2018055999 (print) | LCCN 2019000496 (ebook) | ISBN 9780525656340 (hardcover) | ISBN 9780525656357 (ebook)
Subjects: LCSH: Caro, Robert A. | Journalists—United States—Biography. | Authors, American—20th century—Biography. | Authorship.
Classification: LCC PN4874.C2528 (ebook) | LCC PN4874.C2528 A3 2019 (print) | DDC 818/.5409 [B]—dc23
LC record available at https://lccn.loc.gov/2018055999

Frontispiece photograph:
Arnold Newman Collection / Getty Images
Jacket photograph © Joyce Ravid
Jacket design by Carol Devine Carson

Manufactured in the United States of America
First Edition

For Ina

Beloved

Contents

Introduction

Here's a book very unlike the others I've written—very much shorter, for one thing, as some readers may notice—but its intention is to share some experiences I've had while doing the others, and some thoughts I've had about what I've been trying to do with those books.

It's not a full-scale memoir. I am, in fact, planning to write such a memoir and readers who prefer longer books will not be unhappy with its length. That one will describe in some detail my experiences in researching and writing my biographies of Robert Moses and Lyndon Johnson—my experiences in learning about these two men and their methods of acquiring and using power—and it will describe also the efforts that were made to keep me from learning about these men (or their methods); in writing those biographies, I tried to keep myself out of their narratives, and seem to have done so with such success that over and over again I get asked what it was like to do them. Here, in this current book, instead, are some scattered, almost random glimpses of a few encounters I've had while doing the research on the Moses and Johnson biographies, encounters both with documents and with witnesses. There are also a few things I've learned or discovered, or think I've learned or discovered, about the writing of biography and indeed nonfiction in general that I'd like to share or pass along for whatever they're worth to other writers and to readers interested in nonfiction. And here also are a few things I discovered about myself along the way—starting with a long-ago Election Day in the very tough political town of New Brunswick, New Jersey, when, a wet-behind-the-ears journalist fresh out of Princeton, I found myself "riding the polls" (I didn't even know what the term meant when I was invited to do so) with a very tough old political boss—and about what I wanted to do with my life and my books (which *are* my life): how, for example, a row of tiny dots on a map helped lead me to the realization that in order to write about political power the way I wanted to write about it, I would have to write not only about the powerful but about the powerless as well—would have to write about them (and learn about their lives) thoroughly enough so that I could make the reader feel for them, empathize with them, and with what political power did for them, or to them. It's about what it was like to sit listening to Robert Moses, old but still mighty, what it was like to interview him, to be in a room with him, alone with him (during the brief period, soon to be over, when I was allowed to sit listening to him) and hear him talk about his dreams, the dreams that had become reality, and the dreams that hadn't—yet. It's about what it was like to imagine that I had, during the years I had been a journalist, learned something about how political power worked—and then to realize, as Robert Moses talked, that compared with him I knew nothing, nothing at all; that there was a whole level of political power, not what I had learned from textbooks and lectures in college and not even what I had learned as a political reporter, but a level of which I had hardly ever conceived. And, listening to Commissioner Moses, I learned there was a whole level of ruthlessness, too, of which I also hadn't conceived—learned it the hard way, interviewing the people whose lives he had destroyed, people who lived in the way of his roads, and people—public officials or reformers—who stood in his way period.

THIS BOOK ALSO OFFERS a few glimpses into why I work the way I do—into why, for example, it takes me so long to produce my books. I am constantly being asked why it takes me so long, and when I say that I'm actually a very fast writer, people can barely conceal their disbelief and amusement. Yet when I was working at *Newsday* I was for a time on the rewrite desk, and I was known as a very fast rewrite man. When a murder or a plane crash occurred, I would don my headset as I sat before my typewriter, and reporters on the scene would telephone in to me what was going on, and as I sat there listening to their reports, I could turn out copy at a rate that seemed to astonish some of my colleagues.

When I left *Newsday* to write a book on Robert Moses a change occurred, for, at the beginning of this enterprise, I found myself remembering what R. P. Blackmur, a courtly, soft-spoken southern gentleman, famous at the time as a literary critic, had said to me years before, on the final occasion we met to discuss a short story I had written in his creative writing course at Princeton. We had to write a short story every two weeks, and I was always doing mine at the very last minute; I seem to recall more than one all-nighter to get my assignment in on time. Yet Professor Blackmur was, as I recall, complimentary about my work, and I thought I was fooling him about the amount of preparation and effort I had put into it. At that final meeting, however, after first saying something generous about my writing, he added: "But you're never going to achieve what you want to, Mr. Caro, if you don't stop thinking with your fingers."

"Thinking with your fingers." Every so often, do you get

the feeling that someone has seen right through you? In that moment, I knew Professor Blackmur had seen right through me. No real thought, just writing—because writing was so easy. Certainly never thinking anything all the way through. And writing for a daily newspaper had been so easy, too. When I decided to write a book, and, beginning to realize the complexity of the subject, realized that a lot of thinking would be required—thinking things all the way through, in fact, or as much through as I was capable of—I determined to do something to slow myself down, to not write until I had thought things through. That was why I resolved to write my first drafts in longhand, slowest of the various means of committing thoughts to paper, before I started doing later drafts on the typewriter; that is why I still do my first few drafts in longhand today; that is why, even now that typewriters have been replaced by computers, I still stick to my Smith-Corona Electra 210. And yet, even thus slowed down, I will, when I'm writing, set myself the goal of a minimum of a thousand words a day, and, as the chart I keep on my closet door attests, most days meet it.

It's the research that takes the time—the research and whatever it is in myself that makes the research take so long, so very much longer than I had planned. Whatever it is that makes me do research the way I do, it's not something I'm proud of, and it's not something for which I can take the credit—or the blame. It just seems to be a part of me. Looking back on my life I can see that it's not really something I have had much choice about; in fact, that it was not something about which, really, I had any choice at all.

When I was a reporter, I blamed this feeling on the deadlines. I just hated having to write a story while there were still questions I wanted to ask or documents I wanted to look at. But when I turned to writing books, the deadlines were no longer at the end of a day, or a week, or, occasionally, if you were lucky in journalism, a month. They were years away. But there *were* deadlines: the publisher's delivery dates. And there was another constraint: money—money to live on while I was doing the research. But the hard truth was that for me neither of these constraints could stand before the force of this other thing. It wasn't that I was cavalier about the deadlines. As it happened, I was lucky enough to have a publisher who never mentioned them to me, but they loomed in my mind nonetheless, as I missed them by months and then by years. And I *hated* being broke, having to worry about money all the time. (I didn't know the half of it. It wasn't until, in 1974, when, after I had been working on the book for seven years, *The New Yorker* bought four excerpts from *The Power Broker* that my wife, Ina, said, "Now I can go to the dry cleaners again." I hadn't realized—because she had never told me—that we had been unable to pay the bills at our local dry cleaners (or, I later learned, butcher shop) for so long that she had been doing her shopping in a more distant shopping area. (As, years earlier, we had moved to an apartment in Spuyten Duyvil in the Bronx after I came home one day to the house on Long Island that Ina loved, at a complete loss as to how to go on without a regular paycheck, to find her standing in the driveway to tell me, "We sold the house today.")

But when I began researching Robert Moses' expressway-building, and kept reading, in textbook after textbook, some version of the phrase "the human cost of highways" with never a detailed examination of what the "human cost" truly consisted of or of how it stacked up against the benefits of highways, I found myself simply unable to go forward to the next chapter. I felt I just had to try to show—to make readers not only see but understand and *feel*—what "human cost" meant. And I felt I had figured out a way to do that: to take one mile of the 627 miles of highway that Robert Moses built and show what the building of that mile meant for the thousands of human beings who had lived in the highway's path or adjacent to it. I had selected a mile that I thought would be good for demonstrating this: a mile of the Cross-Bronx Expressway that ran through a neighborhood called "East Tremont." I even knew what I was going to call that chapter: "One Mile." But I wasn't fooling myself: I also knew it was going to take months, perhaps six months, to research that neighborhood—to learn what it had been like before the expressway came, to find (because they were scattered now) and interview people Moses had evicted because they had been in the expressway's path. And also, in order to show what the neighborhood had now become, to interview the people—overwhelmingly black and poor—who had moved into vacated apartments in buildings adjacent to the expressway. (And I knew also that I was going to be frightened sometimes in doing the research; I had spent some days interviewing in East Tremont already, going into buildings where the stench of urine and of piles of feces in corners was so thick in the lobbies that it made your eyes tear, walking up stairs past walls that had been torn open so that people on drugs could get at the copper in the pipes inside; I had already encountered the hostile, menacing stares of the young men standing on street corners eyeing me; had been warned not to be in East Tremont after dark. But the truth was that from the moment I thought of dramatizing the human cost of highways, I just *couldn't* write the book about the great highway builder—couldn't outline it, even—without showing the human cost of what he had done.

I tried to write *The Power Broker* without dramatizing this human cost. I would start outlining the next chapters, to go for-

ward without the East Tremont chapter, and it was as if something in me would rebel, and I would sit there for hours, fiddling
with the outline, knowing it was no good, knowing that if I went
forward, the book behind me wouldn't be the book it should
be, and my heart just wouldn't be in the writing anymore. Lack
of discipline, you might say. Lack of discipline is what *I* said.
But, looking back now, I have to accept the fact that in deciding
to research and write that chapter—as in deciding to research
and write so many chapters that it would have been possible
to publish the books without including; indeed in doing the
books as a whole the way I have done them, taking so long to do
them—there really was no choice involved; that I didn't really
have one.

THERE IS ANOTHER REASON the books take so long—a reason
that has to do not only with my nature but also with what I am
trying to accomplish with those books.

   The original objective when Ina and I moved to the edge of
the Hill Country of Texas in 1978 was to learn about the boyhood and young manhood of Lyndon Johnson. But while I was
interviewing ranchers and farmers, and their wives, about him,
I realized I was hearing, just in the general course of long conversations, about something else: what the lives of the women
of the Hill Country had been like before, in the 1930s and '40s,
the young congressman Lyndon Johnson brought electricity to
that impoverished, remote, isolated part of America—how the
lives of these women had, before "the lights" came, been lives of
unending toil. Lives of bringing up water, bucket by bucket, from
deep wells, since there were no electric pumps; of carrying it on
the wooden yokes—yokes like those that cattle wore—that these

women wore so they could carry two buckets at a time; of doing the wash by hand, since without electricity there were no washing machines, of lifting heavy bundle after bundle of wet clothes from washing vat to rinsing vat to starching vat and then to rinsing vat again; of spending an entire day doing loads of wash, and the next day, since there were no electric irons, doing the ironing, with heavy wedges of iron that had to be continually reheated on a blazing hot wood stove, so that the ironing was also a day-long job, a day of standing close to the stove even in the blazing heat of a Hill Country summer. I was hearing about all the other chores that had to be done by hand because there was no electricity, of all the tasks that made these women old and bent ("bent" being the Hill Country word for "stooped") before their time. It gradually sank in on me that I was hearing a story of a magnificent kind of courage, the courage of the women of the Hill Country, and, by extension, of the women of the whole American frontier. I was trying to use my books to tell the history of America during the years of Lyndon Johnson; this was a significant part of that history, and I wanted to tell it. (*Wanted?* There it was again, same as always. I *had* to tell it, or at least to try.)

It took a long time to learn that story, and I don't think it could have been learned much faster than Ina and I learned it. At the beginning, these women, who lived lives of the deepest loneliness—their homes sometimes at the end of dirt roads on which, you realize, you have driven thirty miles without passing another house; who were so unaccustomed to talking to strangers, particularly about personal matters—weren't giving me the details I needed. Ina solved that. We had three fig trees on our property. Ina taught herself to make fig preserves, and when she started bringing a jar with her as a gift, suddenly these women were her friends, and were showing her—and then, when she brought me back with her, showing me—things I will never forget.

Some of those interviews contained moments of revelation—of shock, really. A woman with whom my earlier conversation had been stilted and unrevealing, this time suddenly blurting out, "You're a city boy. You don't know how heavy a bucket of water is, do you?" Walking over to her garage, she brought out an old water bucket to which a long length of frayed rope was attached, and walked partway down a slope to a well that was covered with wooden boards. Pushing them aside, she handed me the bucket and told me to drop it in. It dropped quite a way. When it seemed full, she told me to pull it up, and I felt how heavy it was, and thought of how many buckets she—mostly she alone, her husband working in the fields or with the cattle all day, her children working beside him as soon as they were old enough, no money on Hill Country farms or ranches to even think of paying a hired man—had to pull up every day. I found a 1940 Agriculture Department study of how much water each person living on a farm used in a day: forty gallons. The average Hill Country family was five people. Two hundred gallons in a day, much of it hauled up by a single person.

And then they had to get the water to the house. It was another elderly woman who asked me, "Do you want to see how I carried the buckets?" I suppose I nodded. Walking over to her garage, she pulled up the door, and there was her yoke. I don't know that I will ever forget that woman—old and frail now, but her shoulders were thin, and her arms, too, you felt, had always been thin—standing there in front of that heavy bar of wood. I don't know whether there might have been a faster way to do the learning for this chapter than the way Ina and I did it, because sometimes with these laconic farm and ranch women, it took several visits before they would relax. It wasn't until I had called on one Hill Country ranch woman several times, I remember, that she said, about washing the clothes, "Oh, did I tell you about the soap? We didn't have enough money for store-bought soap, so we used lye soap that we made ourselves. There was a saying around here: 'Lye soap peels the skin off your hands like a glove.'" And of course, as Ina became friends with them, they told her intimate details that they would never have told me: about the perineal tears, caused by childbirth without proper medical care, which seemed to be common in the Hill Country. (And indeed were: I was looking up federal statistics and studies from New Deal days all the time now, and one study by a team of gynecologists had found that out of 275 Hill Country women, 158 had perineal tears, many of them third-degree "tears so bad that it is difficult to see how they stand on their feet.") And yet, Ina would tell me, her eyes brimming, how these women had told her they had no choice but to stand on their feet and do the chores; with their husbands working "from dark to dark" (that was a phrase Ina and I learned during those three years) there was no one else to do them. I recall many moments of revelation like that; as I say, I hope to write about more of them someday. When Ina said to me one evening with real anger in her voice, "I don't ever want to see another John Wayne movie again," I knew exactly what she meant. So many of the women in Western movies were simply the background figures standing at stoves or pleading with their husbands not to go out to a gunfight. You hear a lot about gunfights in Westerns; you don't hear so much about hauling up the water after a perineal tear. But both acts are equally part of the story, the history, of the courage it took to settle America's frontier. I understood that now, and I remember how badly, when I sat down with my legal pads and my typewriter, I wanted to make others understand it, too. Usually I give Ina my drafts to read only when I've finished a whole section of a book, but I gave her "The Sad Irons" chapter as soon as I pulled its last page out of my typewriter, and I was really proud when she said it was okay.

And here's another thing: I'm not going to suggest that spending those three years learning about the Hill Country was a sacrifice. Getting a chance to learn, being *forced* to learn—really learn, so that I could write about it in depth, so that I could at least try to make it true to reality, to make the reader feel the harshness of the fabric of these women's lives—being given an opportunity to explore, to discover, a whole new world when you were already in your forties, as Ina and I were: that wasn't a sacrifice; being able to do that was a privilege, exciting. The two of us remember those years as a thrilling, wonderful adventure. Writing that chapter, "The Sad Irons," didn't take so long, but researching it did. I cannot pretend that I regret having taken the time.

And there is another reason that my feelings about having taken so much time do not include even a trace of regret. Because for some years following publication of *The Path to Power*, the first Johnson book and the one that contains the "Sad Irons" chapter, I gave talks to conventions or meetings of America's rural electrification associations.

Over and over—in my memory, many, many times—at the end of my talk or during the book-signing that followed, women would approach me. Over and over again I would lean down from the platform or up from the book I was inscribing to hear some version of "I'm so glad you wrote that chapter. My mother used to try to tell me how hard her life had been, but I never really understood. Now I try to tell my daughter how hard her grandmother's life was, and she'll understand because I can give her your book."

Then, after a few years, what I was hearing was "My grandmother used to try to tell me . . ." Now there is no one left to tell the daughters and the granddaughters. The women who lived that life, a life before electricity—millions and millions of them—of course are almost all dead, and they can't tell their story to their descendants. So the story might easily have been lost. If in even small measure I told it for them, these women of the American frontier, and in order to accomplish that, *The Path to Power* took a couple of years longer to write, well—*so what?*

SO IF THIS BOOK is not a full-fledged memoir, what is it? It's a series of pieces, some previously published, some newly written for this book, about my work and how I do it: how I do research in documents; how I report, either on the scene or by interviewing; how I write. The previously published material is drawn from a variety of sources: a piece written for a magazine and a piece written for a newspaper; three parts of the book are adapted from lectures. The new work consists of recollections (recollections in place of a memoir, you could say) about dealings with documents—about how the first piece of advice that I ever got about dealing with them has guided me all my life—and about dealings with witnesses: how I decided there was a person I must talk to, how I found him (not always easy), what it was like to talk to him. (And, in one case, how I was unable, during an entire interview, to bring myself to look at the person who was talking to me.) All these pieces, old and new, have to do in one way or another with method, process, means—the means to an end, the end of course being a book.

The first part of this book, adapted from a lecture, includes a few brief recollections about my time as a newspaperman, among them about that New Brunswick Election Day that made me understand myself a little better; about my first experience going through files, which in a way furthered the understanding; about getting that first crucial piece of advice about how to do that; about being broke while I was writing *The Power Broker*, and about being rescued from being broke.

The second part deals with *The Power Broker*. While I was writing that book, I tried to keep myself out of it. There are a couple of places in the book's narrative in which I had to break that rule in order to make clear where a piece of information came from, but, while I am not going to go back through the book to find every one of those places, I do not believe that the pronoun "I" appears more than a few handfuls of times in its 1,162 pages of text. And except for two paragraphs in the book's "Note on Sources," I did not tell readers what it was like to be sitting there listening to Robert Moses. During the years since the publication of the book, in 1974, I have been asked what that was like so often that when, in 1998, almost a quarter of a century after publication, I was invited by *The New Yorker* to write an article that would include a description of our interviews, I agreed. And now, another two decades later, I'm including that article as part of the second section of this book.

I also include in this second section a conversation, published in *Harper's Magazine*, about my search for Robert Moses' files. And finally an article I wrote for *The New York Times* in 1995, on the occasion of the hundredth anniversary of the New York Public Library, that describes the years I spent in a very special room there while I was writing *The Power Broker*.

The remainder of the book is centered on Lyndon Johnson. In

the third section, newly written, I try to show what went into the gathering of material on the man and his methods, first by giving a few glimpses—just scattered samples, really—into encounters with documents, glimpses that I hope give a feeling of how Ina and I dealt with the vast—forty-five million pieces of paper by the last count—mass of documents in the Lyndon B. Johnson Library in Austin, Texas, as well as with those in the Franklin D. Roosevelt Library in Hyde Park, New York, the Harry S Truman Library in Independence, Missouri, the Dwight D. Eisenhower Library in Abilene, Kansas, the Richard B. Russell Library in Athens, Georgia, the Senate Historical Office in Washington, D.C., the County Clerk's offices in Blanco, Gillespie, Comal, and Hays Counties, the Bexar County Election Bureau in San Antonio, etc., etc., etc.

The fourth section, "Interviewing," also new, is about my encounters with witnesses: about a few interviews I conducted. In order to provide context for what I describe, it has sometimes been necessary to recapitulate material in my four Johnson volumes that deal with the incidents that are being described, but in this book I'm trying to show how the material was gathered: the method, if you will. In doing this, I have also provided, I'm afraid, a few glimpses into me.

The fifth section, part of which is adapted from a lecture I gave at the Leon Levy Center in Biography at the City University of New York, is also centered on Johnson, but this section mainly concerns itself with something I have come to feel is crucial to the writing of biography, and indeed to the writing of history and of nonfiction in general: what I call a "sense of place."

The sixth section, adapted from a lecture, is about the fifth and final book in The Years of Lyndon Johnson, the one I'm writing now about President Johnson, and about the 1960s. I can't discuss that book in any detail here—my writing seems never to come out well if I've talked about it beforehand. That was another thing I learned about myself as a reporter. My first job at *Newsday* was working nights; to get a story "up front" (in the first seven pages of the tabloid), you had to sell it first to the Assistant Night City Editor, then, if he liked it, to the Night City Editor, and then you might also have to discuss it with the Night Editor. By the time I had done all that, I was so bored with the story that I no longer was interested in writing it. So I'm not going to discuss this fifth book in detail; I'll instead talk about two songs that, as I'm working on the book, I've come to feel symbolize the 1960s and the decade's triumphs and tragedies. One, "We Shall Overcome," I've written about before, in the Introduction to Book Two, *Means of Ascent*. The other is "Waist Deep in the Big Muddy."

In 2016, *The Paris Review* printed an interview with me. Some of it replicates material already included in this book, and naturally I omit it here. But other parts of the interview deal with an aspect of my work that I haven't covered—with what for want of a less pretentious phrase could be called my writing process: what hour in the day I start, what hour I finish, how I organize my books and so on. I have been asked, am continually being asked, about how I write. The interviewer for the magazine, a conscientious and thoughtful young man named Jim Santel, asked me the right questions, and I include some of my replies to him as the seventh part of this book.

AND, FINALLY, one more question to answer: why am I publishing this book now, why don't I just include this material in the longer, full-length memoir I'm hoping to write? Why am I publishing these random recollections toward a memoir while I'm still working on the last volume of the Johnson biography, when I haven't finished it, while I'm still—at the age of eighty-three—several years from finishing it?

The answer is, I'm afraid, quite obvious, and if I forget it for a few days, I am frequently reminded of it, by journalists who, in writing about me and my hopes of finishing, often express their doubts of that happening in a sarcastic phrase: "Do the math." Well, I *can* do that math. I am quite aware that I may never get to write the memoir, although I have so many thoughts about writing, so many anecdotes about research, that I would like to preserve for anyone interested enough to read them. I decided that, just in case, I'd put some of them down on paper now.

"Turn Every Page"

P eople are always asking me why I chose Robert Moses and Lyndon Johnson to write about. Well, I must say I never thought of my books as the stories of Moses or Johnson. I never had the slightest interest in writing the life of a great man. From the very start I thought of writing biographies as a means of illuminating the times of the men I was writing about and the great forces that molded those times—particularly the force that is political power.

Why political power? Because political power shapes all of our lives. It shapes your life in little ways that you might not even think about. For example, when you're driving up to the Triborough (now Robert F. Kennedy) Bridge in Manhattan in New York, you may notice that the bridge comes down across the East River in Queens opposite 100th Street. So why do you have to drive all the way up from 100th Street to 125th Street to cross it, and then basically drive back, which adds almost three totally unnecessary miles to every journey across the bridge?

Well, the reason is political power. In 1934, Robert Moses was trying to get the Triborough Bridge built, and he couldn't because there wasn't enough public or political support for the project. William Randolph Hearst, the publisher of three influential newspapers in New York, owned a block of tenements on 125th Street.

Before the Depression, the tenements had been profitable, but now poor people didn't have jobs, and couldn't pay their rent. Hearst was losing money on the buildings and he wanted the city to take them off his hands by condemning them for some project. Robert Moses saw that the project could be the Triborough Bridge, and that's why the bridge entrance is at 125th Street. That's a small way in which political power affects your life. But there are larger ways, too.

Every time a young man or woman goes to college on a federal education bill passed by Lyndon Johnson, that's political power. Every time an elderly man or woman, or an impoverished man or woman of any age, gets a doctor's bill or a hospital bill and sees that it's been paid by Medicare or Medicaid, that's political power. Every time a black man or woman is able to walk into a voting booth in the South because of Lyndon Johnson's Voting Rights Act, that's political power. And so, unfortunately, is a young man—58,000 young American men—dying a needless death in Vietnam. *That's* political power. It affects your life in all sorts of ways. My books are an attempt to analyze and explain that power.

WHEN DID I start writing? It seems to me that I always wrote. I went to elementary school at Public School 93 in Manhattan. It was on 93rd Street and Amsterdam Avenue. It had never had a school newspaper, so when I was in the sixth grade I created one. We mimeographed it. I remember I couldn't get the ink off my hands—I showed up in class with ink all over them.

My mother died when I was eleven, and before she died she told my father that she wanted him to send me to the Horace Mann School. I started there in the seventh grade, and almost immediately I began working on the school newspaper. The paper meant something special. I don't think we were even conscious of what, but we knew. To this day, I have dinner fairly regularly with guys who worked with me on the *Horace Mann Record*.

I always liked finding out how things work and trying to explain them to people. It was a vague, inchoate feeling—I don't think of it in terms of, Why do I want to be a reporter? At Princeton, I was the paper's sportswriter and I had a column, but I found myself writing more about the coach and about how he coached than about how the team was actually doing. I think figuring things out and trying to explain them was always a part of it.

My first job out of Princeton, in 1957, was for a newspaper in New Jersey—the New Brunswick *Daily Home News*, "The Voice of the Raritan Valley"—that was very closely tied to the Democratic political machine in New Brunswick. In fact, it was so closely tied to the machine that its chief political reporter, who was so elderly that he had actually covered the Lindbergh kidnapping in the early Thirties, would be given a leave of absence during the political campaign—that's the chief *political* reporter—so that he could write speeches for the Democratic organization. This reporter suffered a minor heart attack shortly after I got there, so someone else was going to have to write the speeches, and he wanted it to be someone who would pose no threat to his getting the job back later, so he picked this kid from Princeton, and I found myself working for the political boss of New Brunswick, this tough old guy.

For some reason, he took a shine to me. My salary at the paper was fifty-two dollars a week. No specific salary was mentioned when I went to work for him, but every time he liked a speech I wrote he would pull out a wad of fifty-dollar bills and hundred-dollar bills and peel off what seemed like quite a few and give them to me. I was happy with that aspect of the job, but then came Election Day.

He brought me along to ride the polls with him, which meant going from polling place to polling place to make sure that everything was proceeding as it should. But on this particular day the driver of his limousine wasn't the regular driver. The driver had been replaced by a police captain.

I didn't understand why, but as we got to each polling place a policeman would come over to the car, and the captain and my employer would roll down their windows, and the boss would ask how things were going. Usually the answer was everything is "under control." But at one polling place, the policeman said they had had some trouble, but they were taking care of it. And then I saw that there was a group of African-American demonstrators, neatly dressed men and women, mostly young, who had obviously been protesting something that was going on at the polls. And as I watched, police paddy wagons pulled up. There was one there already. And the police were herding the protesters into the paddy wagons, nudging them along with their nightsticks.

The thing that got me when I thought about this in later years—what it was that really hit me—was the meekness of these people; their acceptance, as if this was the sort of thing they expected, that happened to them all the time. All of a sudden I didn't want to be in that big car with the boss. I just wanted to get out.

As I remember it, I didn't say a word. The next time we pulled up to a traffic light, I just opened the door and got out. The boss didn't say a word to me. I think he must have understood. Anyway, I never heard from him again.

But I had realized that I—Bob Caro—wanted to be out there with the protesters.

Not long after that, I decided that if I wanted to keep on being a reporter, I needed—for myself—to work for a paper that fought for things. Why? I couldn't explain it then, and I can't explain it now. But it had to do with that Election Day. With the protesters. With the cops nudging them along with the nightsticks. I had gotten so *angry*!

I looked around for a newspaper that fought for causes. There were several at the time, and I wrote letters to all of them asking for a job. It took a while, but I got an offer from *Newsday* on Long Island—a real crusading paper then—and in 1959 I went to work for them.

Newsday had a managing editor named Alan Hathway, who was an old-time newspaperman from the 1920s. He was a character right out of *The Front Page*, a broad-shouldered man with a big stomach that looked soft but wasn't. His head was shiny bald except for a monk-like tonsure, and rather red—*very* red after he had started drinking for the day, which was at lunch. He wore brown shirts with white ties, and black shirts with yellow ties. We were never sure if he had actually graduated from, or even attended, college, but he had a deep prejudice against graduates of prestigious universities, and during his years at *Newsday* had never hired one, let alone one from the Ivy League. They hired me as a joke on him while he was on vacation. He was so angry that I was there that during my first weeks on the job, he would refuse to acknowledge my presence in his city room. I kept saying, "Hello, Mr. Hathway," or "Hi, Mr. Hathway," when he passed my desk. He'd never even nod. Ignoring me was easy for Mr. Hathway to do because as the low man on the paper's reportorial totem pole, I never worked on a story significant enough to require his involvement. When I had been working on the New Brunswick paper, Ina and I had been living in a garden apartment in Edison, New Jersey, with our baby son, Chase, and we hadn't yet moved to Long Island. I had told Ina we'd better not move; I was probably going to get fired. I drove back and forth to work every day.

Newsday then did not publish on Sundays, so as low man on the totem pole, I worked Saturday afternoons and nights, because if a story came in then, I could put the information in a memo and leave the actual writing of the story to the real reporters who came in Sunday, and would do the writing for the Monday paper. The last of the other reporters and editors would leave about noon on Saturday; for the rest of the day and the evening, I would be alone in the vast, cluttered *Newsday* city room, empty but not silent with the constant ringing of the telephones lined up on the city desk and the ceaseless clatter of the wire machines.

Late one Saturday afternoon, a telephone on the city desk rang, and when I picked it up, it was an official of the Federal Aviation Agency, calling from his office at what was then, because John F. Kennedy hadn't yet been assassinated, Idlewild Airport. *Newsday* had been doing a series of articles on Mitchel Field, a big Air Force base in the middle of Long Island's Nassau County, that the military was giving up. Its twelve hundred acres were the last large open space in the county, so what happened to it was important. The FAA was in the process of ruling that it should become a civilian airport. *Newsday*, however, felt that it should be used instead for public purposes, in particular for education, to allow Hofstra University to expand, and to create a campus for Nassau County Community College, the only public higher education on Long Island, which was then being housed in temporary quarters in the County Courthouse in Mineola. The rooms there were already too crowded to accommodate the students, many from the large low-income community in nearby Hempstead, who wanted a college degree. Public education for the poor, free public education: that was something worth fighting for.

I hadn't been working on any of the Mitchel Field stories. But on this Saturday, suddenly this guy from the FAA was on the phone, and he says something like, "I really like what you guys are doing on Mitchel Field, and I'm here alone in the FAA offices, and if you send someone down here, I know what files you should be looking at, and he can look at them."

I was alone, the only person in the city room. This happened to be the day of the big *Newsday* annual summer picnic on the beach at Fire Island. Just about everyone else had gone, except me. None of them had a cell phone, of course, since there were no cell phones then. I called the editor who was my immediate superior, and then *his* superior, without being able to reach them. When, after many calls, I finally did reach an editor, he told me to call the paper's great investigative reporter, Bob Greene, and have him go down to Idlewild, but Greene wasn't reachable, either, and neither were the other reporters I was told to call. Finally the editor told me that I would have to go myself.

I will never forget that night. It was the first time I had ever gone through files. The official met me at the front door and led me to a room with a conference table in the middle of it, and, on the table, high stacks of file folders. And, somehow, in a strange way, sitting there going through them, I felt at home. As I went through the memos and the letters and the minutes of meetings I could see a pattern emerging of the real reason why the agency wanted the field to become a civilian airport: because executives of corporations with offices on Long Island, who seemed to be quite friendly with FAA officials, wanted to be able to fly in and out of Long Island in their company planes without having the inconvenience of driving to Idlewild or LaGuardia Airports. I kept looking for a piece of paper on which someone came right out and said that, but I didn't find one; everything I could find on paper talked around that point. But between all the pieces of paper, I found sentences and paragraphs that, taken together, made the point clear. I found enough to demonstrate that.

There are certain moments in your life when you suddenly understand something about yourself. I loved going through those files, making them yield up their secrets to me. And here was a particular and fascinating secret: that these corporate executives were persuading a government agency to save them some driving time at the expense of a poor kid getting an education and a better chance in life. Each discovery I made that helped to prove that was a thrill. I don't know why raw files affect me that way. In part, perhaps, because they are closer to reality, to genuineness. Not filtered, cleaned up, through press releases or, years later, in books. I worked all night, but I didn't notice the passing of time. When I finished and left the building on Sunday, the sun was coming up, and that was a surprise. I went back to the office and before driving home, I wrote a memo on what I had found.

Early Monday morning, my day off, the phone rang, and it was Alan's secretary, June Blom. Alan wanted to see me right away, she said. I said, "I'm in New Jersey."

"Well, he wants to see you just as soon as you can get here." I told Ina, with what I suppose was a wry smile, that we had been right not to move. I drove to *Newsday* that morning sure every mile of the way that I was about to be fired.

I ran into June just as I entered the city room; motioning to Alan's office, she told me to go right in. Walking across the room, I saw, through the glass window, the big red head bent over something he was reading, and as I entered his office, I saw that what he was reading was my memo.

He didn't look up. After a while, I said tentatively, "Mr. Hathway." I couldn't get the "Alan" out. He motioned me to sit down, and went on reading. Finally he raised his head. "I didn't know someone from Princeton could do digging like this," he said. "From now on, you do investigative work."

I responded with my usual *savoir faire*. "But I don't know anything about investigative reporting."

Alan looked at me for what I remember as a very long time. "Just remember," he said. "Turn every page. Never assume anything. Turn every goddamned page." He turned to some other papers on his desk, and after a while I got up and left.

ALAN HAD IN FACT heard what I said. A few days later, he called me in and said, "I'll sit you next to Bob Greene." Greene was an already legendary investigative reporter. As I recall, for a while I didn't have any investigative stories of my own, but from those two—Alan and Bob Greene—I learned how to be a reporter. And these weren't lessons you'd be taught in journalism school. One time Bob and I were looking into a phony charitable "cancer research" organization which was spending the bulk of its money on a luxurious lifestyle for the director and his mistress. We had the goods, but we weren't going to be able to use them. We needed an admission from the director, or at least a good comment. We took our material to Alan before we went to interview the director. He said, "When you talk to him, don't sit too close together. Caro, you sit over here, Greene, sit over there. You fire these questions fast—Caro, you ask one; Greene, you ask one—I want his head going back and forth like a Ping Pong ball." It worked: the guy's head kept swiveling, he got rattled, he made a comment I'm sure he wished he hadn't. We had our story.

Another time Alan said about a guy I was investigating and who didn't want to talk to me: "Tell him that if he doesn't, he'll be eating his meals off a tin tray for the next ten years." It sounds funny, but there was a lesson I learned then: When you need to get information from somebody, you have to find *some way* to *get it*.

A FEW YEARS INTO my tenure at *Newsday*, I'd had a few scoops and successes. I'd been nominated for a Pulitzer and had won a couple of minor, I mean really minor, journalistic awards, but when you're young, and you win something, even minor, you think you know everything. I thought I was really something. I thought I knew everything about politics and how politics and political power worked.

Robert Moses wanted to build a bridge across Long Island Sound between Oyster Bay on Long Island and Rye in Westchester County. *Newsday* assigned me to look into it, and I did, and the bridge was a really terrible idea. It would have created even bigger traffic jams—you would have needed something like eight more lanes on the Long Island Expressway just to handle the additional traffic from New England that would have been created. And because the bridge would have been so long, the piers on which it stood would be so large that they actually would have caused pollution along the coastline of Long Island Sound.

Newsday sent me to Albany. The governor was Nelson Rockefeller. I spoke to him. I spoke to his chief counsel. I spoke to the Assembly Speaker. I spoke to the president of the State Senate. Everyone seemed to understand that this bridge was a terrible idea. So I reported back to *Newsday* that the bridge idea was dead and went on to something else.

I had a friend in Albany. A couple of weeks later he called me and said, "Bob, I think you better come back up here."

And I said something like, "Oh, I don't think that's necessary. I think I took care of that bridge."

He said, "Bob, Robert Moses was up here yesterday, and I think you better come back."

So I drove up. I'll never forget this. I walked into the press room to find a stack of press releases from Robert Moses announcing that a "study" of the bridge, an obvious first step toward its construction, would begin immediately—with the participation of the state. And now, when I went back to the same officials who had assured me they were firmly against the bridge, I found there had been a change in their position. They were now firmly for it.

I remember I drove home that night, and all the way down from Albany to our house on Long Island—it was 163 miles—I kept thinking, Everything you've been doing is bullshit. Underlying every one of my stories was the traditional belief that you're in a democracy and the power in a democracy comes from being elected. Yet here was a man, Robert Moses, who had never been elected to anything, and he had enough power to turn around a whole state government in one day. And he's had this power for more than forty years, and you, Bob Caro, who are supposed to be writing about political power and explaining it, you have no idea where he got this power.

And, thinking about it later, I realized: and neither does anybody else.

*

I DIDN'T DO MUCH with this thought at the time. I loved being a reporter, but you're always running from one story to another: There's always a new story. It wasn't until I became a Nieman Journalism Fellow at Harvard that I finally had the time to think. I was already twenty-nine years old. The Nieman fellowship is for mid-career journalists who want to spend a year at Harvard learning more about the areas they cover, and I was taking courses on urban planning. One of my courses was taught by two professors who had written a well-regarded textbook on highways, including an analysis, in great detail, of highway location: why highways get built where they're built. They were doing this by means of a mathematical equation. There were factors such as population density, traffic patterns, elevation of grades—that sort of thing. And at each class they would write the equation on the board, and then they would add new factors to it. And this equation was getting quite long. When I was at Princeton, I was a very diligent note-taker, and I was being a very diligent note-taker in this course and writing everything down. And then one day, while I was taking notes, I suddenly thought, No, that's not why highways get built where they get built. They get built there *because Robert Moses wants them there!*

There were a great many social events for the Nieman Fellows that year. But Ina's mother was very sick, and she had to be home to take care of her, so I was up at Harvard alone a lot of the time, and I've never liked going to social events alone. Harvard had given each of the Nieman Fellows a small office, and I spent a lot of evenings alone in mine. For the first time, really, I had a chance to think about what I had been doing and what I wanted to do with my life. And I guess I came to feel that if I could find out where Robert Moses got his power—this power that no one understood; this power that nobody else was really even thinking about, the power was just sort of there, it had been there for more than four decades—if I could explain it, I would be adding something to the knowledge people ought to have about political power, not the kind of things you learn in a textbook but the raw naked realities of power, about how power works in cities, how it really works.

I knew one book editor in New York, and only one. I wrote him a letter, and I got a contract, a very small contract. It was for $5,000, of which I got $2,500 in advance. And I started out to write a book that turned out to be *The Power Broker*.

WHEN I FIRST BEGAN *The Power Broker* in 1966, since we didn't have any savings to speak of, and we had a son, and my advance was so small that I still needed a weekly paycheck, I convinced myself that I could write the book while continuing to work at *Newsday*. But that illusion didn't last very long. I wasn't making much progress on the book, hardly any progress at all. Then I heard about something called the Carnegie Fellowship in Journalism. They took one working journalist at a time and paid him his weekly salary for a year while he wrote a book. I wrote a letter of application, and I received the fellowship. I quit *Newsday* immediately and told Ina, "They're paying me for a whole year and I have this outline, I'll be done in nine months, and then we can finally go to France." I had always met my newspaper deadlines. And my outline said I'd be done in nine months. At the end of the year, of course, the book was barely started, and we were completely out of money.

For about the next four years money was a problem. As I've said, Ina sold our house in Roslyn, Long Island. We had talked about selling it but in my mind we hadn't finalized it. Ina finalized it. After the mortgage was paid back, we cleared about $25,000, which was enough to live on for a year, and we moved to an apartment in the Bronx that we really disliked. I went around and asked superintendents in the nearby buildings if they had a small room to rent as an office, and found a tiny one, a cinder-block room in a basement, for a little money. When I remember these years, it was a time of just getting by. We didn't go out to eat much. Ina went to work, teaching, for a year, but then I hurt my back playing basketball, and I had to stay in bed for several months. I needed someone to do the research, so Ina would drive out to the Nassau County Courthouse. I'd say you go up to the second floor and there's a phone booth there—I knew this court-house backwards and forwards from my days as a reporter—and call me. She'd call and I'd say now go through the doors right behind you, go in there and they'll ask you so and so, but you want to go to the second row of the file cabinets on the right. I'd tell her that sort of thing. But there came a time when we really totally ran out of money. I just didn't know any place to turn.

By this point, I'd written about half the book, about five hundred thousand words. I gave it to my editor. I didn't hear back from him for a long time. When he did finally call me, he took me to dinner at an inexpensive Chinese restaurant on Broadway. And he basically said, "We've read the manuscript and we like it. Keep going." And I said, "Can I have the other half of my advance?"

There are sentences that are said to you in your life that are chiseled into your memory, and his reply was one. "Oh no, Bob," he said. "I guess you didn't understand. We like the book, but not many people are going to read a book on Robert Moses, and you have to be prepared for a very small printing. We're not prepared to go beyond the terms of the contract." Even I understood that that last sentence meant, You don't get the other $2,500 until you've finished.

That was the worst night. We were really at the end of our rope. I didn't know what to say to Ina. I didn't know how to face her. I remember I walked all the way up Broadway through Harlem and Inwood to our apartment in the Bronx. This was 1971 and Harlem was not a friendly place, but that night that never crossed my mind. I knew I was going to have to go back to work, and it was going to be very hard to finish the book.

By this time I felt, rightly or wrongly, that I had learned some things it was important for people to know. But they were never going to know them if I didn't finish the book. And that night, I just couldn't see any way of finishing it.

Soon after, luckily, things changed. My editor left his publishing house, and there was an "out" clause in my contract saying that I could leave if he left. I knew I needed an agent. I didn't know any agents, but I had a friend who gave me a list of four. Three of them were men, and one was a young woman named Lynn Nesbit. In 1971, awareness of the women's revolution had not yet penetrated to the Bronx, so I went to see the three men first, but they all reminded me too much of myself. In my memory they all wore horn-rimmed glasses, like me, and sports jackets that had elbow patches on the sleeves, or that looked like they *should* have elbow patches on the sleeves. Then I went to see Lynn. I remember sitting across the desk from her, and there was a call she said she had to take. She was selling a Tom Wolfe story to some magazine. And as I listened to her on that call, I said to myself, *that's* what I need.

Lynn had read my manuscript, and said, "I'd like to represent you, but you have to tell me something first. Why do you look so worried?"

I didn't know I *looked* worried. But of course I was. I told her, "I'm worried that I won't have enough money to finish the book." My editor had left me feeling that few people would read a book on Robert Moses, and that therefore no publisher would give me the money I needed to finish it.

She asked how much money I was talking about. I told her I needed enough so I could spend two more years on the book. I thought it would take me two years. I don't remember the exact amount I specified, but I know it was not that large. And all of a sudden there were other sentences that I'll never forget. She said, "Is that what you're worried about? Then you can stop worrying right now. I can get you that by just picking up the phone. Everybody in New York knows about this book."

Then she said, "You can stop worrying about money. But I've read this manuscript. What you care about is writing. My job is to find you an editor you can work with for the rest of your life. I'm going to set up lunches for you"—I think there were four, all with well-known editors—"and you can pick the one you want to work with."

Three of the editors took me to the Four Seasons or some other fancy restaurant, and basically said they could make me a star. Bob Gottlieb at Knopf said, "Well, I don't go out for lunch, but we can have a sandwich at my desk and talk about your book." So of course I picked him.

Robert Moses

The City-Shaper

Beyond Jones Beach, the great park Robert Moses had built
when he was young, was a little private community called
Oak Beach, and Moses said our first interview would be in
his summer cottage there. So I drove out from the Bronx that day
in 1967, over bridges he had built (the Henry Hudson and the
Triborough) after generations of city officials had been unable to
build them, and over expressways he had built (the Cross-Bronx
and the Major Deegan and the Bruckner) by ramming them
straight through the crowded neighborhoods of New York, and
over parkways he had built (the Grand Central and the Cross
Island and the Southern State and the Meadowbrook) when the
most powerful forces in the state had sworn he would never build
them.

When I reached Oak Beach, and turned in through wooden
gates that hung ajar, the colony seemed deserted in the preseason
May chill: the little cottages set among the high dunes were
empty and boarded up, and the narrow, graded road through the
dunes had been covered by drifting sand, so there was no sign
of life. And then I came around a curve. Suddenly, in a circle of
dunes below a modest house was a long, gleaming black limousine, and, beside it, a black-uniformed chauffeur and three
armed and booted parkway troopers. The chauffeur was loung-
ing against the car, but although the troopers, members of an

elite two-hundred-member unit that was in effect Moses' own private police force, were only there on an errand, they stood rigidly erect, as if they feared he might be watching them from the house above.

As I stepped out of my car, a tall woman—his wife—came out on the deck of the house and said that Commissioner Moses was ready to see me, and I climbed the stairs, and, with Mrs. Moses holding the door open, entered a large living room. It was plainly furnished, but most of its far end was glass—a huge picture window. Through the left portion of the window could be seen, about a mile beyond the house, the long low steel roadway and high center arch of the bridge that linked Long Island to the Fire Island barrier beach—the Robert Moses Causeway. Through the right portion could be seen, jutting into the sky, the partially completed two-hundred-foot-high red brick tower that was the centerpiece of the five-mile-long park at the end of Fire Island—the Robert Moses State Park. And in front of the window, in a big easy chair, sat Robert Moses. Looking up at me, framed by his monuments, he said, "So you're the young fellow who thinks he's going to write a book about me," and, standing up, he came toward me with a wide, warm grin on his weathered face.

ALTHOUGH I HAD BEEN working on his biography for almost two years, this was the first time I had met Robert Moses, the man who, more than any other individual, shaped modern New York. Getting to meet him had not been easy. Although he had been the most powerful figure in New York City and New York State for more than forty years—more powerful than any mayor or any governor, or any mayor and governor combined—the only previous "biography" of him was a totally adulatory book written fifteen years earlier under his literally line-by-line supervision. Despite many other attempts, no writer had been able to do another book about him, and when I, then a reporter at *Newsday*, had written him in 1965 to propose the project, I was told that I wasn't going to do one, either. His two top public relations aides, Murray Davis and Edward V. O'Brien, informed me—in two separate conversations, to make sure I got the idea—that I would have absolutely no access to his family, friends, or aides, to any state or city officials, or to his documents, or to him. Therefore, they said, they presumed I would be forgetting the idea of writing a biography of Commissioner Moses. And for almost two years he had, with some success, done his best to make sure that this prohibition stood. He was then at the very height of his power, with absolute discretion over the awarding of contracts by city or state in every field of public works, and the word had gone out that no architect, engineer, or contractor who spoke to me would ever receive another such contract. I had, however, drawn, on a piece of paper, a series of concentric circles around a dot that represented him. The innermost circle was his family, friends, and close associates, and I was prepared to believe that he could keep me from seeing them, and probably the persons in the next circle or two, also. But surely, I felt, there would be people in the outer circles—people who knew him but were not in regular contact with him—who would be willing to talk to me. And, in fact, there were, and, as I was later to be told, Commissioner Moses was more and more frequently encountering people who, unaware of his feelings, said that this young reporter had been to see them. I was, moreover, spending a lot of time going through documents, including the papers of Moses' great patron in the 1920s, Governor Alfred E. Smith, in the New York State Archives in Albany, and nothing that went on in Albany escaped his notice. And one day in May, 1967, Moses' daughter Jane had telephoned me to say that "Papa Bear" would see me. The aide closest to him, Sidney M. Shapiro, later told me the reason for his change of heart—or, at least, a reason. Because Mr. Shapiro and I were eventually to spend a great deal of time together, and he appeared to regard me with affection, this explanation may be too complimentary to me; however, no one ever gave me any other. He said that "RM," learning of my stubbornness despite his strictures, had concluded that at last someone had come along who was going to write the book whether he cooperated or not.

I HAD FIRST BEEN drawn to Robert Moses out of curiosity, in a very idle, fleeting form. As a new reporter at *Newsday* during the early 1960s, I would, as the occupant of an extremely low rung on the city room totem pole, occasionally be assigned to write a short article based on one of the press releases that poured in a steady stream from one or another of the twelve governmental entities he headed, and as I typed "New York City Park Commissioner Robert Moses announced today . . ." I would wonder for a moment what that title had to do with the fact that he was also building something that was not a park—and was mostly not even in the city—the Long Island Expressway. I would type "Triborough Bridge and Tunnel Authority Chairman Robert Moses" and it would cross my mind that he was also chairman of some other public authority—actually, the New York State Power Authority—that was building gigantic hydroelectric power dams, some of the most colossal public works ever built by man, hundreds of miles north of the city, along some place with the romantic name of the "Niagara Frontier." It gradually sunk in on me that in one article or another I was identifying him as chairman or "sole member" of quite a few authorities: the Bethpage State Park Authority, the Jones Beach State Park Authority, the Henry Hudson Parkway Authority, the Marine Parkway Authority, the Hayden Planetarium Authority—the list seemed to go on indefinitely. And as, within a few months of my coming to *Newsday*, my interest began to narrow to politics, I began to wonder what a public authority was, anyway. They were always being written about simply as nonpolitical entities that were formed merely to sell bonds to finance the construction of some public work—a bridge or a tunnel, usually—to collect tolls on the work until the bonds were paid off, and then to go out of existence, and, in fact, a key element of the image of Robert Moses that had for forty years been created and burnished by him and by an adoring press was that he was the very antithesis of the politician, a public servant uncompromisingly above politics who never allowed political considerations to influence any aspect of his projects. After all, the reasoning went, he built most of his projects through public authorities, which were also outside politics.

No journalist or historian seemed to see authorities as sources of political power in and of themselves. I remember looking up every article on public authorities that had been written in newspapers, magazines, and scholarly journals for some years past; there was not one that analyzed in any substantial way the potential in a public authority for political power. Yet, in some vague way, they certainly seemed to have some. Moreover, Robert Moses held still other posts—city posts, such as New York City Construction Coordinator, and chairman of the city's Slum Clearance Committee; and state posts, such as chairman of the

State Council of Parks, and chairman of the Long Island State Park Commission. I began to feel that I was starting to glimpse, through the mists of public myth and my own ignorance, the dim outlines of something that I didn't understand and couldn't see clearly but that might be, in terms of political power, quite substantial indeed.

THEN I WAS DRAWN to Robert Moses by my imagination—by an image that lodged in it, and grew vivid. The more I thought about Robert Moses, and about the power he exerted, and about my ignorance—and, it seemed to me, everyone's ignorance—concerning the extent of his power, and the sources behind it, the more apparent it became to me that trying to determine the extent and identify the sources, and then to explain what I found, was something beyond the scope of daily journalism; no newspaper, in the journalistic practices of that day, would give you the time to conduct such an exploration or the space to print what you found.

It would be necessary to do a book. And, while I was trying to decide whether I really wanted to write one on Robert Moses, I began reading material about him, and one of the things I read, in a typescript in the Columbia University Oral History Collection, was the oral history of Frances Perkins, who would later be Franklin Roosevelt's secretary of labor but in 1914 was a young reformer, who often spent her Sundays walking around New York City with another young reformer, Robert Moses.

Born on December 18, 1888, to a wealthy German Jewish family active in the settlement house movement, Moses had been educated at Yale and Oxford, and had returned to New

York to earn his Ph.D. in political science at Columbia and join a municipal-reform organization as a researcher. In 1914, at the age of twenty-five, he was filled with idealism—he had devised an elaborate plan to cleanse New York of Tammany Hall's influence by eliminating patronage from the city's corruption-ridden civil service system—and with ideas, many of them about public works. "Everything he saw walking around the city made him think of some way that it could be better," Miss Perkins had told her oral-history interviewer. "He was always burning up with ideas, just burning up with them!"

The biggest idea of all concerned the western shoreline of Manhattan Island from about Seventy-second Street up to about 181st Street. That six miles of shoreline, below the high cliff of Riverside Drive, was popularly called Riverside Park, but, unlike the park's landscaped upper level, in 1914 the part along the edge of the Hudson was nothing more than a six-mile-long wasteland of mud and rapidly eroding landfill, and through its entire length ran four tracks of the New York Central Railroad, bordered by high, sharp-edged fences that for seventy years had cut the city off from its waterfront. Since the locomotives that towed the endless trains carrying cattle and pigs south to the slaughterhouses downtown burned coal or oil, the "park" seemed constantly covered with a thick, gritty, foul-smelling black smog. Huge mounds of raw garbage lay piled there, waiting for scows to collect it and carry it out to sea. There were several large shantytowns in it, inhabited by derelicts so intimidating that their shacks were avoided even by the police; at night, the residents of Riverside Drive apartment houses could see the derelicts' open fires glowing in the darkness by the river. But one Sunday in 1914, as a group of young men and women were taking a ferry

to a picnic in New Jersey, Robert Moses was standing beside
Frances Perkins on the deck, and as the ferry pulled out into the
Hudson, and the bleak mudflats shrouded in smog spread out
behind them, he suddenly said excitedly, "Isn't this a temptation
to you? Couldn't this waterfront be the most beautiful thing in
the world?" And, Miss Perkins was to recall, he began to talk,
faster and faster, and she realized, to her amazement, that "he
had it all figured out. How you could build a great highway that
went uptown along the water. How you'd have to tear down a
few buildings at Seventy-second Street and bring the highway
around a curve," how the railroad tracks would be covered by the
highway, and cars would be driving serenely along it with their
passengers delighting in the river scene, how there would be long
green parks filled with people playing tennis and baseball and
riding bicycles, and elegant marinas for sailboats.

Looking up from the typescript (bound, I still remember, in a
gray loose-leaf notebook), I realized that what Robert Moses had
been talking about on that long-ago Sunday was what I knew as
Riverside Park and the West Side Highway—the great park and
road that, as long as I could remember, had formed the western
waterfront of Manhattan Island. Although many other plans had
been conceived for the waterfront, this immense public work
would be built by him—in 1937, almost a quarter of a century
after the ferry ride. And it would be built—this urban improvement on a scale so huge that it would be almost without prec-
edent in early-twentieth-century America, this improvement that
would, in addition, solve a problem that had baffled successive
city administrations for decades—in very much the same form
in which he had envisioned it as a young municipal reformer just
out of college.

At the same time, moreover, from other oral histories, and

brief references in articles, I was learning *how* Robert Moses had envisioned it—where he was standing when he did so, even what he might have been wearing. He lived then with his parents on Central Park West, but often, after work, he would tell his taxi driver to take him instead to Riverside Drive, at the end of Seventy-sixth Street, overlooking the Hudson. And then, as the sun set behind the Palisades across the river, he would get out and stand staring down at the smog-covered wasteland below him. He was a striking young man—tall, very slim, darkly handsome, with olive skin and deep, burning eyes, elegant and arrogant—and fond of white suits, wearing them from early spring well into the autumn. And he was passionate when, defending his plan for civil service reform, he talked night after night before hostile, Tammany-packed audiences, speaking into storms of invective—so passionate that another reformer was to say, "Once you saw him on those nights, you could never forget him." In my mind, I saw him now, staring down in the evenings on the Hudson waterfront, and I couldn't forget him. Sometimes, in my imagination, I saw him from below—a tall, handsome, haughty figure in white, standing on the edge of a high cliff and gazing down on a vast wasteland with the eyes of a creator, determined to transform it into something beautiful and grand. Sometimes, I saw him from behind—a tall black silhouette against the setting sun. Robert Moses gazing down on Riverside Park lodged in my imagination and, in my imagination, became entangled in a mystery: I had previously been aware only of the Robert Moses of the 1950s and '60s: the ruthless highway builder who ran his roads straight through hapless neighborhoods, the Robert Moses of the Title I urban-renewal scandals—some of the biggest and most sordid scandals of twentieth-century New York, scandals almost incredible both for the colossal scale of their corruption (personally "money honest" himself, Moses dispensed to the most powerful members of the city's ruling Democratic political machine what one insider called "a king's ransom" in legal fees, public relations retainers, insurance premiums, advance knowledge of highway routes and urban renewal sites, and insurance-free deposits in favored banks, to insure their cooperation with his aims) and for the heartbreaking callousness with which he evicted the tens of thousands of poor people in his way, whom, in the words of one official, he "hounded out like cattle." Now I saw something very different: the young Robert Moses, the dreamer and idealist. How had the one man become the other?

AND, FINALLY, I was drawn to Robert Moses by something that wasn't imagination at all but, in some ways, its opposite: by an insight, a hard, cold, and, I believed, rational calculation about what I wanted to do with my own work, and how it was through Robert Moses that I could do it.

As I began, little by little, to understand the magnitude of his impact on New York, I was beginning to feel that he could be a vessel for something even more significant: an examination of the essential nature—the most fundamental realities—of political power.

One of the reasons I believed I had become a reporter in the first place was to find out how things really worked and to explain those workings, and, as my focus had narrowed to politics, that reason had become to explain how political power really worked. And during the few years I had been a reporter I had convinced myself, in part because of the easy gratifications that go with the journalist's life—the bylines; the gratitude or the wary respect or fear that the subjects of your articles had for you; the awareness of friends or neighbors of what you were doing; the feeling that you were at the center of the action—that I was succeeding in doing what I had set out to do.

But the more I thought about Robert Moses' career, the more I understood that I had been deluding myself. In the terms in which I had always thought about New York politics, elected officials—mayors and governors in particular—were the principal repositories of the political power that plays so significant a role over our lives: in a democracy; after all, ultimate power theoretically comes from the ballot box. But Robert Moses had never been elected to anything. And yet Robert Moses had held power for forty-four years, between 1924 and 1968, through the administrations of five mayors and six governors, and, in the fields in which he chose to exercise it, his power was so enormous that no mayor or governor contested it. He held power, in other words, for almost half the century that began when, on January 1, 1898, the five boroughs were united into a single city (which became, with that unification, the greatest city in the New World). And during that century he, more than any mayor or governor, molded the city to his vision, put his mark upon it so deeply that today, fifty years after he left power, we are still, to an astonishing extent, living in the city he shaped.

The legislative act that unified New York created a city of five boroughs, but only one of them—the Bronx—was on the mainland of the United States, so the new city was really a city of islands. It was Robert Moses, more than any legislature or any other individual, who tied those islands together with bridges, soldering together three boroughs at once with the Triborough

Bridge (and then tying two of them, the Bronx and Queens, even more firmly together with the Bronx-Whitestone and Throgs Neck Bridges), spanning the Narrows to Staten Island with the mighty Verrazano, tying the distant Rockaways firmly to the rest of the metropolis with the Marine and Cross-Bay spans, uniting the West Bronx and Manhattan with the Henry Hudson. Since 1917, seven great bridges have been built to link the boroughs together. Robert Moses built every one of those bridges.

He built every one of the expressways that cut across the city, carrying its people and its commerce—fifteen expressways, plus the West Side Highway and the Harlem River Drive. If a person is driving in New York on a road that has the word "expressway" in its name, he is driving on a road built by Robert Moses.

He built every one of the parkways that, within the city's borders, stretch eastward toward the counties of Long Island, and he built every one of the parkways that, beyond those borders, run far out into those counties, thereby shaping them as well as the city. There are eleven of those parkways in all. And he either built or rebuilt—rebuilt so completely that they became largely his creations also—five parkways stretching toward, or within, Westchester County, so that he built a total of sixteen parkways. In New York City and its suburbs, he built a total of 627 miles of expressways and parkways.

He created—or re-created, shaping to his philosophy of recreation—every park in the city, adding twenty thousand acres of parkland (and 658 playgrounds) in a city that had been starved for parks and playgrounds; since he left power, several new parks have been built, and several older parks—most notably Central Park—have been restored to their pre-Moses form, but most of

New York's parks are still, today, essentially the parks of Robert Moses. And for the use of the city's residents he created, outside the city's borders, on Long Island, another forty thousand acres of parks, including not only Jones Beach, which may be the world's greatest oceanfront park and bathing beach, but other huge parks and beaches—Sunken Meadow, Hither Hills, Montauk Point, Bethpage, Belmont Lake, Hempstead Lake, and eight others.

And bridges, roads, parks, and beaches are only a part of the mark that Robert Moses left on New York. During the time in which he controlled—controlled absolutely—the New York City Housing Authority, the authority built 1,082 apartment houses, containing 148,000 apartments which housed 555,000 people: more people than, at the time, lived in Minneapolis. Those apartments are mainly for persons of low income. For persons of higher income, he created, under urban-renewal programs, tens of thousands of additional apartments. He was the dominant force, moreover, behind such supposedly "private" housing developments as Stuyvesant Town, Peter Cooper Village, Concord Village, and Co-op City—and such monumental features of the New York landscape as Lincoln Center, the United Nations headquarters, Shea Stadium, the New York Coliseum, and the campuses of Fordham, Pratt, and Long Island Universities. He changed the city's very shape, enlarging it by adding to its shoreline more than fifteen thousand acres of new land, tying together small islands within its borders with rock and sand and stone, so that, for example, Ward's Island and Randall's Island were united, and Hunters and Twin Islands were joined to Rodman's Neck, so that their combined area would be big enough to hold the mile-long crescent of his Orchard Beach creation. He built public works that, even in 1968 dollars, cost $27 billion (a figure that would have to be multiplied many times to put it in today's dollars). He was the greatest builder in the history of America, perhaps in the history of the world.

He shaped the city physically not only by what he built but by what he destroyed. To build his expressways, he evicted from their homes 250,000 persons, in the process ripping out the centers of a score of neighborhoods, many of them friendly, vibrant communities that had made the city a home to its people. To build his non-highway public works, he evicted perhaps 250,000 more; a 1954 City Planning Commission study of just seven years of Robert Moses' eviction policy was to call it "an enforced population displacement completely unlike any previous population movement in the City's history." And, since the people he evicted were overwhelmingly black, Hispanic, and poor, the most defenseless of the city's people, and since he refused, despite the policy of the city's elected officials, to make adequate provision (to make any substantial provision at all, really) for their relocation, the policies he followed created new slums almost as fast as he was eliminating old ones and, tragically, were to be a major factor in solidifying the already existing ghettoization of New York—the dividing up of its residents by color and income.

Immense as was Robert Moses' physical shaping of New York, however, his influence on the city's history cannot be measured merely by the physical. All told, during the decades of his power he used that power to bend the city's social policies to his philosophical beliefs, skewing, often despite the wishes of its mayors and other elected officials, the allocation of the city's resources to the benefit of its middle, upper-middle, and upper classes at the expense of the city's lower middle class and its poor, and particularly at the expense of the new immigrants. These were blacks and Puerto Ricans, mainly, who had begun arriving in New York in substantial numbers not long after he came to power in the city. His power also has to be measured by zoning policies on Long Island that guaranteed suburban sprawl, and by decades of systematic starvation of the subways and commuter railroads that he viewed as rivals for his roads and the revenue they produced, a policy that exacerbated the highway congestion that has made traffic jams an inescapable part of New Yorkers' lives.

The more I thought about Robert Moses' career, the more I realized that his story and the story of New York City were, to a remarkable degree, one story.

And the more I thought about Moses' accomplishments, the more I realized that I had no idea—as, apparently, no one had any idea—of what the political power was that had enabled him to achieve them, of how he had acquired that power, or, aside from the sketchiest details, of how he had used it. And therefore I came to feel that if what I had for so long wanted to do was to discover and disclose the fundamentals of true political power—not theoretical political power but the raw, naked essence of such power—then perhaps the best way to do that was through portraying the life of Robert Moses.

WHATEVER THE REASON, or reasons, that he finally agreed to see me, my interviews with Robert Moses—there would, over the next year, be seven of them; long interviews, one lasting from nine-thirty in the morning until well into the evening—were worth any trouble it had taken to get them. They were less interviews, perhaps, than monologues. Questions were not encouraged. I would raise a subject, and Moses would thereupon embark on a discourse about it that might take an hour or more, and if I attempted to interrupt to clarify a point, the interruption might or might not be acknowledged.

But, at least at first, who wanted to interrupt? I had thought I understood something—had thought I understood quite a bit, in fact—about the inner processes of political decision-making, and about urban planning and government in general. From the moment Robert Moses started talking, I never thought that again.

He seemed to remember every vote—even votes from forty years before—and why it had been cast. "On the Jones Beach appropriation, it was eight to seven against us in Ways and Means," he would say. "But the key was this little upstate guy [and he named some long-forgotten state assemblyman], and he had a mortgage coming due on his farm, and the mortgage was held by a bank up there, and the key to the bank was Hewitt [Charles J. Hewitt, chairman of the Senate Finance Committee], and the governor knew how to get to Hewitt, so it was eight to seven for us."

He seemed to remember every decision, and how decisions had been changed—how, for example, the use of liquor had been helpful in effecting some changes, particularly during the Prohibition Era, with upstate Republican legislative leaders who liked to drink but who would never be forgiven by their rabidly dry constituents should it be learned that they did so, and who were therefore all the thirstier at the weekend parties that Al Smith, the Democratic governor, threw for them at the Long Island sites for which Moses wanted legislative appropriations ("They hated my guts," Robert Moses told me, with that wonderful smile. "But they all loved the governor, so they came"), and at which, as

Moses put it, sitting in front of the big window, "we fed them liquor."

One such reception was attended by the State Senate Majority Leader, John Knight, who had been blocking Moses' appropriations for two years; who during the just completed 1925 legislative session had accused Moses, his voice shaking with rage, of "lawlessness and a violation of sacred constitutional property rights"; and who, when a reporter asked him if there was any possibility of his relaxing his opposition in future sessions, had replied, "I don't change my mind very often, do I?"

"We were opening a bathhouse at Sunken Meadow," Moses recalled. "We had cases of Scotch and bourbon that we were feeding to the fellows and Knight disappeared." Trying to enter the bathhouse, Moses said, he had found the door jammed, and when he finally pushed it open he discovered that what had been blocking it was Knight, who was sitting on the floor, dead drunk, trying to hold the door shut with his foot while he poured "a whole bottle" down his throat. "I said, 'You lousy bastard.' He was so embarrassed he didn't know what to say"—and thereafter, if Knight didn't formally change his mind, his fear of exposure led him to drastically soften his opposition.

Moses remembered subtler, and more brutal, means of decision-changing, too. Once, in an infrequent interruption, I asked him about one of Mayor Robert F. Wagner's deputy mayors, Henry Epstein. Epstein had long been a Moses ally. "A very able lawyer," Moses had said earlier. "Outstanding lawyer. I had known him a long time." But in 1953 Epstein was standing in Moses' way, telling Mayor Wagner that there was no rational reason for Moses to shove the Cross-Bronx Expressway through the East Tremont neighborhood of the Bronx on a route that, in just one mile, would require the demolition of fifty-four separate apartment houses when there was another, parallel route, which would require the demolition of exactly six small brownstone tenements, just two blocks away. And then Epstein had abruptly changed his mind, and had written a letter to Wagner saying he had been wrong and that Moses' route was better.

I asked Moses why Epstein had changed his mind.

He changed it, Moses said, "after he was hit over the head with an axe."

When I asked him what he meant, he said, "I won't tell you what we did to him." But in the course of the interview he did tell me, if obliquely.

He had, he said, put "our bloodhounds"—the team of investigators who compiled the dossiers on other city officials which Moses leaked to newspapers if an official opposed him—on Epstein. And then, he said, he had had a talk with Epstein, who was married, and the conversation had included some references to a woman. "A lot of personal stuff got into it," Moses recalled. "I said, 'This woman, this chum of yours.' He said, 'She's not my chum.' I said, 'Oh, yes, she is. She's your chum, all right.'

"So," Robert Moses said, with his broad, charming smile, "Henry wrote his letter."

AND HE REMEMBERED things a lot bigger than votes, or decisions, and in the remembering taught me about something much larger than the workings of politics: about a particular type of vision, of imagination, that was unique and so intense that it amounted to a very rare form of genius—not the genius of the poet or the artist, which was the way I had always thought about genius, but a type of genius that was, in its own way, just as creative: a leap of imagination that could look at a barren, empty landscape and conceive on it, in a flash of inspiration, a colossal public work, a permanent, enduring creation.

As I had thought about Robert Moses gazing down at Riverside Park, my imagination had been filled with the picture of Robert Moses as dreamer. Now Robert Moses taught me about dreams, all right, including a dream much bigger than Riverside Park. Suddenly coming up out of the big chair, seizing my arm in a grip that belied his seventy-eight years, he drew me out of the Oak Beach cottage, down the steps, and up to the top of a sand dune, from which I could see down the Great South Bay and the barrier beach. "There was nothing there then," he said. "Nothing." And, standing there on the dune, a broad-shouldered old man with very young gray eyes, the wind whipping his sparse white hair around his olive face, Robert Moses told me how he had first thought of a park on Jones Beach.

In 1922, Al Smith, who had rescued him from oblivion—four years before, at the age of thirty, Robert Moses, his dreams for Riverside Park and civil service reform shattered, was standing on line outside the city hall in Cleveland, Ohio, applying, in vain, for a minor municipal job; it was the next year that Smith gave him his first taste of power—had assigned Moses as his "observer" at the Good Government organizations that wanted parks outside the cities for the urban masses who suddenly, with the advent of mass-production technology and the resultant shorter workweek, had leisure time to enjoy the countryside and, with the invention of the Model T Ford, automobiles to get to it. No one in the United States, however, seemed able to conceive of parks large enough, or of means to get people to them, and on the mainland of Long Island the problem seemed particularly insoluble. Virtually every foot of desirable beach-front was in the hands either of local municipalities, determined to bar them to the city's immigrant "foreigners," or of America's robber barons, who had established their great strongholds on the Island's Gold Coast. Their immense wealth had brought them immense political power, and on Long Island the roads were kept deliberately narrow and unpaved. But during the summer of 1922 Robert Moses had rented a vacation bunga-low in Babylon, on Long Island's South Shore, and had, he told me now, "fallen in love" with "the bay, with the whole South Shore." Purchasing an old, broad-bottomed, very slow motor-boat, partly covered with an awning—a vessel his wife named the *Bob*—he spent the summer exploring the bay, often so lost in reverie that he would forget time and tide, and find himself stranded on a sandbar. He told me how sometimes he would sail over to the barrier beach ("about over there," he said, pointing down the bay), which was then just a strip of dunes and beach grass and wild marshes about five miles offshore (it had been named after a seventeenth-century privateer, Major Thomas Jones) and looked like a low line on the horizon, and he would pull the *Bob* ashore and step out.

Often, when he did so, he would step into a world in which there was not a single other person in sight. All there was, stretching before him for miles until it disappeared at the hori-zon, was that strip of spotless white sand, sloping on one side into the ocean, rising on the other into low dunes separated by long grayish green marshes. Something in that wild, desolate, barren scene attracted him; he must have returned to it, he said, a hundred times, pulling his little boat through the reeds, to sit alone on the beach. And then one day, he told me, he realized with a jolt that the spot on which he was sitting—this spot so cut off from the rest of the world—was less than twenty-five miles from Times Square. If a park could be built on that spot, the masses of New York City would have, at a stroke, a great bathing beach. All that was needed was a road to bring people out there from the city. He told me that at first the problem of acquiring from hostile Long Island the right-of-way for such a road seemed insuperable, but that he was commuting to Babylon that summer on the Long Island Rail Road and he had suddenly noticed that between some of the villages there were thick bands of woods. He told me how one weekend he went to Babylon Town Hall and asked what the woods were, and found that they were New York City's old, long-unused "reservoir properties," and realized that they were therefore publicly owned, not by Long Island municipalities but by New York City itself, and realized that if the road ran through them much of the right-of-way wouldn't have to be purchased or condemned. And, since one of the properties—the one at Wantagh—ran all the way down to the bay; another road, connecting with the road coming out from New York, could be built south down to the bay without any purchase or condemnation at all. And, since the bay was so shallow, it ought to be easy to construct a causeway from the end of the road to the barrier beach. "That was the idea behind Jones Beach and the Southern State Parkway," Robert Moses told me. "I thought of it all in a moment." Standing there beside me, the wind whipping his hair, the grip on my arm still tight, the gray eyes burning, he was young again, the youthful visionary who had dreamed a dream of a beach and a park and a parkway system greater than the world had ever seen.

*

THE GENIUS OF WHICH he was giving me an understanding was, furthermore, a genius vast in scope—a creative, shaping imagination on a scale so colossal that individual projects, even projects as monumental as the West Side Highway or Jones Beach, were only details within its sweep, an imagination broad enough so that it could take as its medium an entire city and the city's far-flung, sprawling suburbs, and not just a city but the greatest city in the Western world: New York, Titan of cities.

Two of my interviews with Robert Moses were conducted in an office he had on Randall's Island—where he was also framed in a big window by one of his monuments, this one the toll plaza of the Triborough Bridge—and dominating that office was an immense map of the New York region. When he began talking to me about his accomplishments and his plans for future accomplishments, he often stepped out from behind his desk and stood in front of the map, pointing at the relevant places with a sharp-pointed yellow pencil in his hand, and, standing there, he was the artist in front of his canvas. The pencil would make big, sweeping gestures over the map, or sharp, precise jabs toward it: "You see, if we put the road there, there'll be room for parks there and there—see that, just a ribbon park, but big enough to do the job—and over there we'll have room for the baseball diamonds, and if we do that, then the housing can be here . . ." The canvas was gigantic—a metropolitan region of twenty-one hundred square miles in which there lived in 1967 fourteen million people. And the pencil waved over all of it at once as he discussed Staten Island and Suffolk County, Manhattan and Montauk, SoHo and Scarsdale, in the same sentences. I realized that the man standing before me saw the whole canvas—city, suburbs, slums, beaches, bridges, tunnels, airports, Central Park and vest-pocket parks—as one, a single whole, which he wanted to shape as a whole. When Robert Moses talked like that, standing in front of his beloved map, I was as thrilled as Frances Perkins must have been thrilled that day on the ferry, and I understood better the mind that could look down from Riverside Drive on a mudflat and see a great highway and a great park. I also understood better the mind of a sculptor who wanted to sculpt not clay or stone but a whole metropolis: I saw the genius of the city-shaper.

When he talked, moreover, you saw how the dreams—and the will to accomplish them—were still burning, undimmed by age. Often, when Robert Moses sat reminiscing to me at Oak Beach, he did so half turned away from me in the big chair, staring out the long picture window. I had thought he was staring at the bridge named after him and the park named after him—at the things he had accomplished.

Then, one day, he started talking about the park, and said that the thing to remember about it was that it was just "a gateway . . . to other areas." I realized that he was talking about a highway—a four-lane highway atop an eighteen-foot-high dike—he wanted to build the length of Fire Island, from Robert Moses State Park, at its western end, to Smith Point, near its eastern end—some twenty miles—where it would link up with another big causeway that would carry it back to the Long Island mainland, where it would run through the Hamptons and all the way out to Hither Hills and Montauk State Parks, which he had created during the 1920s. Intense opposition from Fire Island communities—opposition entirely understandable, since the broad highway would destroy the very qualities of peacefulness and beauty that made the narrow island precious to its residents—had stopped the project some years before, and the communities believed it had been stopped permanently.

That, however, I now realized, was not Robert Moses' opinion. "The road is going to come," he said firmly. "It's *got* to come."

Looking at me, he saw, I guess, that I was unconvinced, and stood up and walked out onto the deck facing the park and Fire Island, gesturing to me to come with him, and, standing there, pointing at Fire Island, he began to explain that the twenty miles of road on Fire Island was an integral part of something much bigger: a great Shorefront Drive, all the way from Staten Island to Montauk Point—a distance of 160 miles—which he had planned in 1924. Parts of that drive—expressways on Staten Island, the Verrazano-Narrows Bridge, the Belt Parkway, in Brooklyn, the Ocean Parkway along Jones Beach—were already built, but there were still gaps, including that gap on Fire Island.

And then Robert Moses saw that I still wasn't agreeing, and he whirled on me. Suddenly you forgot the paunch and the liver spots. All you could see were those eyes. He grabbed my right arm above the elbow. To this day, I can feel the grip of those fingers as Robert Moses, shoving his face close to mine and glaring at me, said, *"Can't you SEE there ought to be a road there?"* Driving home that night, I realized that when Robert Moses was looking out the window at the bridge and the park he hadn't been thinking about them—about the things he had built.

He had been thinking about the things he hadn't built.

He had unveiled a plan of bridges, tunnels, expressways, parkways, and parks for the metropolitan region almost forty years earlier, on February 25, 1930, when, before five hundred civic leaders assembled in the Grand Ballroom of the Hotel Commodore for the Park Association's annual dinner, he pulled a drape away from a huge map of New York City hanging behind the dais—a map covered with red lines indicating highways and bridges and tunnels, and green areas representing tens of thousands of acres he wanted to acquire for new parks. For almost forty years, he had been filling in that map, turning lines into concrete, green ink into green spaces. But in 1967 his outline was still far from completed. He had built a network of great urban roads—far more urban roads than any other man in history—but there were gaps in that network: gaps on Manhattan Island, where a Lower Manhattan Expressway, across Broome Street, and a Mid-Manhattan Expressway, across Thirtieth Street (an eight-lane highway a hundred feet in the air, above some of the busiest streets in the world, through a forest of skyscrapers), and an Upper Manhattan Expressway, at 125th Street, would, he was sure, solve the metropolitan region's worsening traffic congestion, and other gaps, like the one on Fire Island. On that porch, I had felt the force of the determination of this seventy-eight-year-old man to fill in those gaps. Since he had decided to cooperate with me, he had let it be known that others could talk to me, too, and now I found it easier to believe that they had not been exaggerating when they described the savage energy Robert Moses had put behind his dreams, and his fury when they were checked: how, mapping out strategies for overcoming obstacles, he would pace back and forth across his office, hour after hour; how the palm of his big right hand would smash down, over and over again, on the table as he talked; how he would lunge out of his chair and begin, as one aide put it, "waving his arms, just wild," pick up the old-fashioned glass inkwell on his desk and hurl it at aides so that it shattered against a wall; how he would pound his clenched fists into the walls hard enough to scrape the skin off them, in a rage beyond the perception of pain.

*

DURING THE SAME MONTHS in which I was interviewing Robert Moses, however, I was interviewing people whose lives had been touched by Robert Moses.

Some of them were in the East Tremont neighborhood, with whose fate Henry Epstein had been involved.

One of the implications of Robert Moses' career that I was examining was the human cost of the fifteen massive expressways he had built within the city itself. What had been the effect of these giant roads on the neighborhoods in their paths, and on the residents of these neighborhoods? I had decided to try to show this by focusing on one neighborhood, and had selected East Tremont, through which, during the 1950s, he had built the Cross-Bronx Expressway on that route which had demolished a solid mile of six- and seven-story apartment houses—fifty-four of them—thereby destroying the homes of several thousand families, although there was available just two blocks away the parallel route that would have required the demolition of only six tenements—but which would have also required the demolition of the "Tremont Depot" of the Third Avenue Transit Company, in which several key Bronx Democratic politicians had hidden interests, and which they didn't want condemned.

Up until the day—December 4, 1952—on which the eviction notices signed by "Robert Moses, City Construction Coordinator" and giving the recipients ninety days to move, arrived, East Tremont had been a low-income but stable community of sixty thousand persons, predominantly Jewish but with sizable Irish and German populations. Its residents had been poor—pressers, finishers, and cutters in the downtown garment district—and their apartment houses were old, some without elevators and almost all with aging plumbing. But the rooms were big and high-ceilinged—"light, airy, spacious" was how the residents described them to me—and the apartment houses were precious to the people who lived in them, because, rent-controlled as they were, their residents could afford, so long as they kept them, to live in their community. As long as they had those apartments, they had a lot—a sense of community and continuity; in some of those buildings, two and three generations of the same families were living; young couples who moved away often moved back. "The reason we moved back to that area was that we loved it so much," said one young woman who had moved back shortly before the notices came. "There was no reason for an older person to be lonely in that neighborhood," said one who lived there. If they lost their apartments, they knew, they could not afford to live in the city, and would be scattered to the winds. And then the notices from Moses arrived. "It was like the floor opened up underneath your feet," one woman told me. "There was no warning. We just got it in the mail. Everybody on the street got it the same day. A notice. We had ninety days to get out. . . . We all stood outside—'Did you get the letter?' 'Did you get the letter?' Three months to get out!" (There was no need for such haste: construction of the East Tremont section of the expressway would not, as Moses was aware, begin for three years. The ninety-day warning was merely "to shake 'em up a little and get 'em moving," a Moses aide explained to me.)

The community tried to fight. It was an era before community protests became newsworthy, and the protests they made received scant notice in a press that in those days did not give much space to such protests, but they fought hard, led by a young housewife, Lillian Edelstein, who had never imagined herself in such a role but felt she had no choice ("What if we were separated? What would Mom do? . . . I was fighting for my home. And my mother. And sister. And daughter. I had a lot to fight for") and who turned out to possess not merely energy and determination but an indefinable, and inspiring, air of command. And since every one of their elected officials—their assemblyman and their state senator, as well as Bronx Borough President James J. Lyons and Mayor Wagner—was, at first, on their side, they thought they had a chance. In the New York City of the 1950s, however, when it came to the construction of large-scale public works projects, what counted was not what elected officials wanted but what Robert Moses wanted, and in a very short time the residents lost—and Moses immediately began to apply the "relocation" techniques he had perfected on other projects.

As soon as the city Real Estate Bureau took title to the buildings, the heat and the hot water were cut off in many of them, and for much of the ensuing winter the only warmth for the families trying to remain in their apartments came from small, inadequate electric heaters they themselves bought or gas ranges turned on all the time. The building superintendents had been fired, so there were no services. Some of the tenants began to move, and as soon as the top floor of an apartment house was empty, the roof and that top floor would be torn off. "While people were still living in it, they were tearing it down around their heads!" Mrs. Edelstein told me. When an apartment on a lower floor was vacated, its windows were boarded up—a signal to looters that there were empty premises to be broken into. All requests for watchmen, as for heat and hot water and superintendents, were referred by the city agencies to Moses, who simply ignored them. The looters came: at night, the remaining tenants could hear them tearing the pipes out of the wall to be sold for scrap. A few small frame houses that were on the route were torn down, and their lumber stacked in their backyards—and fires were set. When the first apartment houses were completely emptied, their basements were left as gaping pits filled with broken glass and jagged shafts of steel. Despite parents' pleas, no fences were built around them, and the parents lived in fear that their children would fall into them. Demolition on so immense a scale had other consequences—"The rats were running like dogs and cats in the street," Mrs. Edelstein was to recall. Grime filled the air so thickly that sometimes the neighborhood seemed to have been hit by a dust storm.

In a very short time, the fifty-four buildings were gone. Then, after construction started, there came month upon month and year after year of earthshaking dynamite blasts, since the expressway was, in that neighborhood, being cut through a trench in solid bedrock. The air was filled with rock dust from the great excavation—a deep gash in the earth a hundred and twenty feet wide and a mile long, through which rumbled mammoth earthmoving machines and herds of bulldozers and dump trucks—and the gritty dust seeped into rooms even through doors and windows that had been closed and sealed with towels. East Tremont had, of course, been cut in half by the road, and the southern half was isolated from the shopping area along East Tremont Avenue, and it was hard for the remaining residents to get to stores. The residents of the apartment houses that bordered the mile-long excavation on both sides—perhaps one hundred buildings—began to move out, and as more and more moved one of the principal reasons for staying—friends who lived near you—began to vanish, and so did the sense of community. Still more tenants disappeared from East Tremont. Some landlords were happy to see them leave the rent-controlled apartments, and replaced them with welfare families, who demanded fewer services and moved more often, so that rents could be raised more often. The gyre of urban decay spiraled and widened, faster and faster, and more and more residents began to move. East Tremont became a vast slum.

I spent many days and weeks, terrible days and weeks, walking around that slum.

I had never, in my sheltered middle-class life, descended so deeply into the realms of despair. When I entered these buildings, on the floors of their lobbies would be piles of animal or human feces, and raw garbage spilling out of broken bags; the floors were covered so thickly with shards of broken glass that my feet would crunch on it as I walked. The walls would have been broken open and the pipes ripped out, for sale by junkies. An atmosphere of fear hung over East Tremont, of course. I remember one elderly man, with a kindly face, sitting on a stoop; "You're going to be out of here by dark, aren't you?" he asked me. When he feared he hadn't made himself clear enough, he added, "Don't be around this place after dark!" I remember the people who lived in these buildings: almost all were black or Hispanic. Wanting to interview them to find out what living in East Tremont was like, I would knock on the doors of apartments. Over and over again, in my recollection, the same scene would be repeated. At my knock, there would be a scurry of children's feet behind the door, but no reply. If I persisted in my knocking, I would hear footsteps coming to the door, and then a voice—in my recollection it was always the voice of a little boy—would ask, through the closed door, the same question: "Are you the man from the welfare?" Usually, when I said I wasn't, the door wouldn't be opened. Sometimes, however, it was, and I would be allowed inside—and sometimes that was worse. To this day, I see, in my mind, a black woman, about thirty years old, sitting with several little children around her; no matter what question I asked, she replied, "I've got to get my kids out of here. I've got to get my kids out of here."

If the days I spent interviewing residents of the great East Tremont slum were terrible, the days I spent interviewing former residents of East Tremont—people who had lived there before it became a slum—weren't much better. These people had lived in East Tremont when it had been a neighborhood, their neighborhood, and they had been driven away by Robert Moses, either by the demolition of their homes or by the neighborhood's consequent deterioration. Their stories, too, were part of the human cost of this highway; and I wanted to find as many of them as possible and interview them.

I found them in a great variety of locales. Some—the luckiest or the most affluent ones—had found apartments in sterile high-rise middle-class housing developments in far reaches of the Bronx. Some, less affluent, were living in small—in many cases, too small—apartments in various neighborhoods in the Bronx or in Queens or in Brooklyn. Others were living with their children in the Westchester or Long Island suburbs. And still others, the unluckiest, had come to rest in "the projects," the city's immense, low-income, and quite dangerous public housing.

I asked these couples—or widows or widowers—to compare their present lives with the lives they had had in East Tremont, and the general picture that emerged from their answers was a sense of profound, irremediable loss, a sense that they had lost something—physical closeness to family, to friends, to stores where the owners knew you, to synagogues where the rabbi had said Kaddish for your parents (and perhaps even your grandparents) as he would one day say Kaddish for you, to the crowded benches on Southern Boulevard where your children played baseball while you played chess: a feeling of togetherness, a sense of community that was very precious, and that they knew they would never find again.

And when I tried, just briefly and very gingerly, to raise the issue of human costs with Robert Moses, there was a certain offhandedness in his reply.

The day before this interview, I had spent several hours talking to an elderly couple who were living in a very small apartment in another section of the Bronx. When I asked them how life was now, there had been a long pause, and then the wife had said, "Lonely." There had been a silence; there wasn't too much I could say to that. And then the husband had chimed in with a word, and it was the same word: "Lonely."

Raising the subject of East Tremont with Commissioner Moses, I asked him the most innocuous question I could think of: Wasn't it more difficult to build an expressway in the city rather than a parkway in the country? He waved his hand dismissively: "Oh, no, no, no," he said. "There are more people in the way—that's all. There's very little real hardship in the thing. There's a little discomfort, and even that is greatly exaggerated."

Then I asked him if he had ever been worried about losing to the people up there—of having to change his route to save their homes.

"Nah," he said, and I can still hear the scorn in his voice as he said it—scorn for those who had fought him, and scorn for me, who had thought it necessary to ask about them. "Nah, nobody could have stopped it." In fact, he said, the opposition hadn't really been much trouble at all. "[They] just stirred up the animals there. But I just stood pat, that's all." He looked at me very hard to make sure I understood, and, intending to return to the subject in more depth at some future date, I said that I did.

DURING THOSE SAME MONTHS in which I was interviewing Robert Moses, however, I was also going through papers: the files of Governors Alfred E. Smith and Franklin Delano Roosevelt, of Fiorello La Guardia and other mayors; and the private papers of reformers, urban planners, and politicians who had been involved with Moses in one way or another, years or decades before.

Some of the files had lain untouched for decades, since, at the end of a governorship or a mayoralty or a private career, they had been packed away: Some of the papers of Al Smith had been kept in envelopes, and occasionally when I opened an envelope and unfolded the pages within, they crumbled in my hand, so long had it been since they had been unfolded. And while much of what Robert Moses had been telling me not only was fascinating but was confirmed by the information in those files, on some points—including some crucial points—there were rather sharp discrepancies between his accounts and the written record, so it was necessary for me to start asking him to reconcile his account with that record.

One striking discrepancy concerned two curves in the Northern State Parkway, which Robert Moses had been building eastward out through Nassau and Suffolk Counties in 1929 and 1930, during Roosevelt's governorship. In two spots—Old Westbury, in Nassau County, and Dix Hills, in Suffolk County—the parkway swerved inexplicably south toward the middle of the island before, on the far, or eastern, side of those areas, it curved back and resumed its eastward course. Moses, who during his entire career had eloquently and persuasively portrayed himself as uncompromising—as a public servant who was above politics and would never compromise with what he felt was right—had used the Northern State Parkway to demonstrate that point in his interviews with me. He had told me, quite eloquently, that its route was the one he had originally chosen, that he had refused to compromise over that route—a statement that, of course, meant that the two curves had always been planned.

In going through files, however, I had come across maps showing the proposed parkway without those curves—maps on which the parkway, in a substantially different route from the one it actually followed, ran in a generally straight line through the beautiful hills in the northern part of Long Island. And in Roosevelt's papers I had also come across a series of letters and telegrams that had been sent to him during 1929, the first year of his governorship.

One letter was from Grenville Clark, a noted attorney, who was representing the Old Westbury robber barons in their fight to keep Moses' parkway, and the city masses the barons despised, away from their estates. It referred, in obscure terms, to an arrangement between Moses and the multimillionaire Otto Kahn, which, Clark wrote, on March 29, 1929, if "finally brought to light will not make a creditable chapter in the history of this State." Other letters and telegrams I came across, in various files, showed that Clark was not exaggerating. They revealed that the Northern State Parkway had originally been supposed to run through the middle of an eighteen-hole private golf course that Kahn had constructed for his pleasure on his Dix Hills estate. In 1926, the legislature was refusing to allocate funds to Moses for any purposes connected with the parkway, so that he didn't even have enough money for surveys. The letters showed that Kahn had offered to secretly donate $10,000 to the Park Commission for surveys, provided that some of the surveys found a new route for the parkway—one that would not cross his estate at all. And they revealed that Moses had secretly accepted the money, had used it for surveys, and had indeed found a new route—one that avoided Kahn's estate. South of Kahn's estate lay the estates of other powerful rubber barons, so the route was shifted south again—more than three miles south—so that it ran down the center of Long Island, through a group of small farms.

Clark delivered an ultimatum to Roosevelt, telling the governor that if the parkway's route was not changed to avoid both estate areas, in Old Westbury as well as Dix Hills, the public would be informed of how a millionaire had given $10,000 to keep his private golf course untouched and how Moses had accepted the money and used it to throw farmers off their land. Moses thereupon agreed to a "compromise," which was not really a compromise at all but a complete surrender, under which the parkway would make the two southward curves, so that it would avoid the estate areas, and under which Moses also agreed that instead of building parks along and at the end of the Northern State Parkway, as he had originally planned, there would not be a single park anywhere along that parkway, or anywhere in the section of the North Shore that the barons controlled, so that their Gold Coast would remain undefiled by the city masses. And, in return, the Kahn-Moses transaction was kept secret—and it had remained secret, when I came upon it, for almost forty years.

When the time came for my seventh interview with Robert
Moses—on April 27, 1968—I knew I could no longer postpone
asking him about the arrangement with Otto Kahn. And there
were many other questions that my research had raised about
which I had to ask him—hundreds of questions, really.

I got to ask him only one, however.

I worded my first question about Kahn and the Northern State
Parkway as politely—and, indeed, as obliquely—as possible, but
Robert Moses' mind worked very fast, and I was later to con-
clude that with my very first mention of Kahn's name he knew
that I had seen the crucial letters and telegrams. I could see his
eyes harden. There was not a word of verbal reaction; he simply
changed the subject and, very shortly thereafter, said he would
have to cut the interview short that day.

Every time, during the remaining five years I was working on
The Power Broker, that I tried to arrange another interview, his
secretaries said he was busy; and I never talked to him again.

WHILE MY INTERVIEWS with Moses were over, however, my
research was not. I decided to try to find the farmers through
whose land the parkway had finally run, to see if they could cast
any additional light on the subject.

Finding them was not easy: Though the huge estates of
the great barons were all labeled by name on Moses' maps
(famous names: not only Kahn but Whitney, Vanderbilt, Phipps,
and Morgan, among others), the farms, being much smaller,
appeared on the map as mere dots or slivers; there wouldn't
have been room for names even if someone had wanted to put
them there. And during the forty years since their land had

been taken most of the farmers had died or moved away. When I did find them—to be more accurate, when *we* found them: Ina, the only researcher I had on *The Power Broker* (and the only researcher I have had on all my books), and I each tracked down several of the farmers or their children—I didn't learn anything new about the Kahn-Moses transaction. In fact, they had never heard of it; they believed that the parkway had come through their farms solely because of the reason that Moses' representatives had given them—that engineering considerations made the route the only one feasible.

I did, however, learn about *them*.

I will never forget talking to Helen Roth, the widow of one of those farmers, James J. Roth, and to her son, Jimmy.

As I was asking Mrs. Roth and her son about the parkway's route, Jimmy started talking also about the parkway's effect—on their lives—and after a while his mother, in a very soft voice, chimed in.

When James and Helen Roth bought their farm—forty-nine acres in Dix Hills—in 1922, much of it had been covered with woods, and all of it had been rocky. It had had to be cleared, and since Roth's team of horses couldn't budge many of the stumps, he—and, many times, his wife—pulled beside their horses, hauling at the ropes, while their son, as soon as, at the age of five, he was old enough to do so, handled the team, sitting on one of the horses and kicking him forward. By 1927, however, the land was finally cleared, and despite their discovery that the soil on the southern fifteen acres of the farm would never be any good for planting, the remaining thirty-four acres were rich and fertile. Life was grueling for all three members of the family: there was no money for a hired man. At harvest time, Roth, who had been up before dawn working in the fields, would load up one of his two wagons and drive to market while Helen and Jimmy loaded the other. Every minute mattered to a man trying to work thirty-four acres without a hired man, and so when Roth returned he would hurriedly unharness the team, hitch it to the loaded wagon, and drive to market while Helen and Jimmy reloaded the first wagon. But by 1927 the farm had finally begun to pay. "We felt pretty secure," Jimmy said. "We had a nice farm. In those days, a farm wasn't just real estate, like it is now. In those days, a farm was your living. It was your home. And we had a nice farm."

And then, in 1927, after Moses struck his deal with Otto Kahn, one of Moses' aides drove up to the Roths' farm one day and told them that the Long Island State Park Commission was condemning fourteen acres from the center of the farm for the Northern State Parkway. Taking fourteen acres from the farm's center meant taking fourteen of the farm's only thirty-four fertile acres. And cutting the farm in half with a parkway meant that getting from one half of the farm to the other would require driving off the farm to the nearest road that crossed the parkway; thereby making it far more difficult to work the part of the farm that remained. There was, however, a solution that would not hurt the Roths nearly so much: moving the parkway four hundred feet south—less than a tenth of a mile. If the Long Island State Park Commission did that, the land taken would be taken from the barren part of the farm, and, since that land wasn't worked much anyway, the splitting of the farm by the parkway wouldn't matter nearly so much.

James Roth pleaded with Moses' representative to take that route. All he was asking, he said, was that the road be moved less than a tenth of a mile; that wouldn't matter to drivers using the road—and it would lessen the harm not only to his farm but to all the other farms involved. Moses refused even to consider the plea, saying that the route had been determined by engineering considerations that could not possibly be changed.

"My father was really rocked by this," recalled Jimmy Roth, who as a little boy had sat on a horse watching his father's and mother's backs bent into the ropes. "And I don't know that I blame him. I'll tell you—my father and mother worked very hard on that place, and made something out of it, and then someone just cut it in two." The fourteen acres were condemned; the condemnation award "never came to much," Mrs. Roth said. And since the farm now consisted of two separate, rather small pieces instead of a single big one, they couldn't even sell it.

Working the farm, moreover, became much harder. It took the Roths at least twenty-five minutes to get their team to the nearest road that crossed the parkway and then double back to plow the other side of the farm. Each round-trip took about fifty minutes, and these were fifty-minute segments chopped out of the life of a man to whom every minute counted. "It was quite a ways," Mrs. Roth said, in her quiet voice. "It was quite a ways for a man who was working hard already."

Many other farms—twenty one in the Dix Hills area alone (I don't think I ever counted the ones in the Old Westbury area, but there seem to have been more than twenty-one there)—were similarly ruined by the Northern State Parkway: To those farmers, the day they heard that "the road was coming" would always be remembered as a day of tragedy. One consideration alone made the tragedy more bearable to them—their belief that it was necessary, that the route of the parkway had been determined by those ineluctable engineering considerations. But I knew, from the telegrams and letters, that it hadn't been necessary at all. It would, in fact, have been easy to move the parkway. Besides, for men with power or the money to buy power, Robert Moses had already moved it. It was running across James Roth's farm only because Otto Kahn hadn't wanted it to run across his golf course, and could pay to make sure it wouldn't, and because the Whitneys and the Morgans had power that Moses had decided to accommodate rather than challenge. "For men of wealth and influence," I was to write, Moses "had moved it more than three miles south of its original location. But James Roth possessed neither money nor influence. And for James Roth, Robert Moses would not move the parkway south even one-tenth of a mile farther. For James Roth, Robert Moses would not move the parkway one foot."

I can't honestly say, particularly after so many years have passed, that it was during my conversations with the farmers and with the people of East Tremont that my concept of the kind of book I wanted to write changed. I don't really remember exactly when it changed. But these conversations with the Long Island farmers had brought home to me in a new way the fact that a change on a map—Robert Moses' pencil going one way instead of another, not because of engineering considerations but because of calculations in which the key factor was power—had had profound consequences on the lives of men and women like those farmers whose homes were just tiny dots on Moses' big maps. I had set out to write about political power by writing about one man, keeping the focus, within the context of his times, on him. I now came to believe that the focus should be widened, to show not just the life of the wielder of power but the lives on whom, and for whom, it was wielded; not to show those lives in the same detail, of course, but in sufficient detail to enable the reader to empathize with the consequences of power—the consequences of government, really—on the lives of its citizens, for good and for ill. To really show political power, you had to show the effect of power on the powerless, and show it fully enough so the reader could feel it.

AT THE TIME of my last interview, although I didn't know it then—and I'm not sure Robert Moses fully realized it, either, though the realization was starting to sink in—he was being removed from power, in a vicious struggle with Governor Nelson Rockefeller, who had succeeded, on March 1, 1968, in merging Moses' Triborough Authority into his newly formed Metropolitan Transportation Authority.

Moses believed (as did others involved in the negotiations) that, in return for his support of the merger, Rockefeller had firmly promised him that he would retain all his old power over Triborough within the new agency, and that in addition he would be put in charge of projects he had long been planning, most notably the huge Sound Crossing, a six-mile-long bridge he wanted to build across Long Island Sound between Oyster Bay and Rye in Westchester County; the next (but not the final) link in the chain of bridges—the Triborough, the Whitestone, the Throgs Neck—joining Long Island with the mainland which he had planned decades before. But as the months passed, and the only position Moses was offered with the MTA was a "consultantship," and as the bridge, despite repeated assurances by the governor, remained unauthorized, I realized that Robert Moses' days of power were over, and to the complex mixture of my feelings about him was now added a wholly new one: pity. For, as one of his secretaries, Harold Blake, told me, "He had just as much energy as ever. And what was he going to do with it now?" An architect who knew him well, Arnold Vollmer, said, "The idea of this great mind having nothing to do—that's the most awful thing." And his wife, Rebekah Vollmer, who also knew Moses well, said, "It's horrible. For him, that would be hell." I had gotten to know Robert Moses well enough to know that last statement was true.

During the next five years, as I continued to work on my book about him, he continued to fight and scheme to get power back, swallowing his pride to go hat in hand to Nelson Rockefeller, rallying his allies among the contractors and labor unions who were realizing that the city could not build big jobs without him. ("They want him to get tired and to go away and get lost," Peter Brennan, of the Building and Construction Trades Council, reported to me. "But I say, 'Forget it! This guy don't blow away!'") Although he shrank in height, his physical vigor was still remarkable. (In 1969, a *Daily News* reporter wrote, "He's a big man, not so much in height and weight as in presence, and even now, on the eve of his eighty-first birthday, he's got enough vitality and power to become the instant center of attention when he walks into a room. . . . Even now, it's easy to see why they called Robert Moses a giant.") But all his fighting and scheming was for nought, and when I heard from some of his assistants, still cooperating with me, about how the old man would pace the deck outside the Oak Beach house for hours, staring across at Fire Island, I would feel like crying, as sometimes I felt like crying about the people the old man had crushed when they stood in his way: He never got to build anything again.

When my book, *The Power Broker,* was published, in 1974, he issued a thirty-five-hundred-word statement attacking it—and me—written with all his acerbic brilliance of phrase. In one place, he said: "Charges of arrogance, contempt for the so-called democratic process, lack of faith in plain people, brutal uprooting and scattering of those in the way are as old as recorded history: In such periods, the left wingers, fanatical environmentalists and seasonal Walden Ponders have a field day." He never ceased denouncing me, in speeches and countless letters. He died on July 29, 1981, at the age of ninety-two. Although I wanted very much to attend his funeral, I felt that his family and friends would not want me to be there, so I didn't go.

The New Yorker, January 5, 1998

Carbon Footprint

Conversation between Robert A. Caro and John R. MacArthur,
marking the fortieth anniversary of The Power Broker

CARO: By the time I started the book, Robert Moses had been in power for almost half a century. Moses' people said to me: "He'll never talk to you. His family will never talk to you. His friends will never talk to you. Anyone who ever wants a contract from this city or state will never talk to you."

Worse, they said I could never see any of his papers. Moses had seen to it that they had been closed to the public and the press for forty years. So I was never going to get to see them. This was an even bigger handicap. It's hard to do the kind of book I wanted to do—a book that would explain Moses' methods of getting and using power—without written documentation.

One day I got a call from a wonderful journalist named Mary Perot Nichols, who had been an editor at *The Village Voice* and was then the director of communications for Thomas Hoving, one of Moses' successors as park commissioner. She called me out of nowhere. We'd met maybe two or three times, when we were both covering the New York World's Fair in 1964–65. But apparently—she told me this later—she'd been watching my work at *Newsday*.

"I hear you're doing a book on Robert Moses," she said.

"And I hear you can't see his papers." I told her that was right. She said, "Well, he forgot about the carbon copies."

Moses had been park commissioner for almost thirty years. The commissioner's office is at the Arsenal in Central Park, but Moses hated to go there because there was no private entrance. When he was going upstairs to his office, the other employees could talk to him, and he really didn't like people talking to him. So he ran the Parks Department from his real office, which was on Randall's Island. There's a building underneath the toll plaza of the Triborough Bridge, and that was his headquarters. No one could talk to him there unless he wanted to talk to them.

He ran the Parks Department by communiqué, and he would send carbon copies of the communiqués to the Arsenal. He went to a lot of trouble to make sure that other caches of his papers were brought to Randall's Island, but he forgot about the carbon copies. Mary said, "I know where they are and I can get you a key."

If you go to the 79th Street Boat Basin—I think it's two levels down, but I haven't been there in so many years—there is an area that had been designed as a parking garage for Parks Department trucks. As I remember it, it was a huge empty white space. When I went there for the first time, I turned the key and tugged the door open, and it's a huge garage. But there are no trucks. I turned on the light—they had just a couple of bare bulbs—and there against the far wall was this entire row of four-drawer file cabinets containing not just carbons but thirty years of memos, orders, and directives from Robert Moses to the Parks Department.

Ina and I spent several months going through those papers. This was the era before Xerox. We had a primitive copying machine. It was heavy. So we would park in a lot by the river, and we'd go down to this garage every day carrying this copying machine together. I would take notes, and when I wanted something copied, we'd copy it.

Now, the parkies—these guys in their green Parks Department uniforms, we called them parkies then—they didn't know what I was doing there, exactly, but they vaguely knew it was something that the commissioner, as they all still referred to him, wouldn't like. So whenever we went out—if we went for lunch, or if we both went out to the bathroom or something—they would unscrew the light bulbs. It would be pitch-black when we got back. After a while Ina and I would arrive in the morning, and I'd have a packet of four light bulbs in my attaché case.

MACARTHUR: Imagine trying to do the book without those carbons.

CARO: It wasn't only those papers. There are other collections of papers. I found a memo that showed how Moses used public works to create and wield power. To us, a public work—a bridge, let's say—is a transportation device. To Robert Moses, a bridge was also a source of power. Every aspect of it was a source of power. For example, there was no terrorism then; the Triborough Bridge was not going to fall down. There's no risk. Whoever got to write the insurance policies on the structure would make a lot of money. So Moses would parcel out the policies to politicians who were insurance brokers on the basis of how many votes they controlled in Albany. I found memos in the Moses file that said just that: Jim Roe [a Democratic boss in Queens] has twelve votes in Albany. Give him 18 percent of the insurance premiums. So-and-so controls three votes. Give him 4 percent of the premiums. That sort of thing.

MACARTHUR: And you couldn't have written that without those memos?

CARO: I'd been told about his method of using every aspect of a public works for power. But it would have been very hard to prove. I wouldn't have used it in the book unless I had something in writing. People ask why these books take so long. Over and over you hear about some collection of written documents, and you have to try to find them. You know, you put it together from so many different places. But you always needed something in writing.

In the latter chapters of the book, I write about how Moses threw people out of their homes to build his highways. I was able to get a pretty good conservative figure: about 250,000 people. He threw out about the same number for his "urban renewal" slum-clearance projects. So he threw about half a million people out of their homes. But it was hard to document. It wasn't so hard to document for the highways, because the federal government required some sort of documentation. But for the slum clearance, the federal government didn't require anything.

Moses would just take a site, like the area between Central Park West and Amsterdam Avenue between 97th and 100th Streets. He called it a slum, but it wasn't even a slum. It was a mostly poor but vibrant, bustling black and Puerto Rican neighborhood. And he simply threw the people out.

That was in the Fifties. I wrote the book in the Seventies, and the people were gone. It was really hard to find them. And when you ask people about things that happened a long time ago, their memories are bad, they exaggerate. But I found that there was in fact a written record. I kept finding references to the Women's City Club, whose members had interviewed people as they were losing their homes. Volunteers would do interviews with the people who lived in these apartments, and they would go back to the office and type them up.

Because of those interviews, I was really able to paint a picture. What I found out was that Moses' guys would just tack a piece of paper on the door that looked like an official court notice, saying you had thirty days to get out. It wasn't a court notice but it was designed to look like one. People who had lived in these apartments for years and had no money to move were suddenly told they had thirty days to get out. Then there would be successive notices. You have two weeks, ten days, whatever, to get out. They thought these were official. Once I had these interviews, with their contemporaneous impressions, I could track down these people and go to them and say, "Tell me more."

Harper's Magazine, December, 2014

Sanctum Sanctorum for Writers

Recently, walking into the main entrance of the New York Public Library for a ceremonial occasion, I was directed up the stairway to the left. I found myself, however, walking past the stairs, to a corridor behind them. Set into the corridor's marble wall was a double door of dark wood, tall and forbidding, no lettering on it to identify it, and I stood in front of it, remembering when I had a key to that door—and when that key was one of my most precious possessions.

For some years, in fact, that key—a key to the library's Frederick Lewis Allen Memorial Room, a marble and wood-paneled space containing eleven cubicles for writers—was almost a talisman to me, a charm I clung to during those years to try to make myself believe that the biography of Robert Moses on which I was working might actually become a book.

Before I was admitted to the Allen Room in late 1971, it had become harder and harder for me to believe that. I had been working on the Moses biography for about five years. I had begun it because I felt that an examination of Moses' life would throw new light on the true nature of urban political power and on the history of a great city. As year followed year, and I learned more and more about Moses' life, I became more and more convinced that the book could indeed do that. But, as year followed year, the project had, in my mind, taken on an air of unreality.

In part, this was due to the lack of any relationship between writing the book and the inescapable realities of the rest of life, such as earning a living. While I had, in 1966, been given a book contract, the advance I had received was $2,500, and it had been spent so long ago that it seemed to have no connection with the years that had passed since I received the check. I had been a reporter on *Newsday*, and as Ina, my wife, and I watched our savings run out, and we sold our house to keep going, and the money from the sale ran out—and my editor assured me that while my early chapters appeared to have literary merit, there would be so little audience for a book on Moses that the printing would be modest indeed—the book sometimes seemed more and more like a rather unreal interlude in my life.

I had always believed I was a writer, but to me being a real writer meant writing more than one book, and I could see absolutely no way of getting to write another one. I was determined to finish this one, no matter what. But the only future I could see after that was to try to persuade *Newsday* to rehire me. And it was becoming harder and harder to cling to my image of myself as a writer. My editor, the only editor I knew, seemed to be taking longer and longer to answer my telephone calls. My connection with my publishing house seemed extremely tenuous.

These factors were changing, however. I had acquired an agent and was switching publishers, was being brought together with a very different type of editor, Robert Gottlieb of Knopf, who was trying to find some kind of mechanism that would allow me to stop worrying constantly about money (and who even liked the title, "The Power Broker"). But these changes did not yet seem real to me, and while some things were getting better, what had not gotten better at all was what I have since realized was the most fundamental reason for the feeling of unreality: that I had, for five years, been living in a world utterly unpopulated by anyone else who was doing what I was doing.

As a reporter, my days had been filled not only with bylines, a weekly paycheck and other trappings that made the journalistic world real, but also with interaction with my editors, with other reporters, with the subjects of my articles. When I had a problem connected with my work, there were many people with whom to discuss it.

When I left *Newsday*, I entered a world that was very different, and not just because, instead of seeing my writing in print every day, there had been, in 1971, no writing of mine in print for five years. Following the sale of our house on Long Island, Ina, our son, Chase, and I moved to an apartment in Spuyten Duyvil, in the Bronx. There were certainly other writers in Spuyten Duyvil, but we didn't meet any of them. I don't think that during the first five years I was working on *The Power Broker* I had any contact with a single other writer of serious books. There was no writer with whom I could discuss a writing problem.

By the time I was admitted to the Allen Room, moreover, my feelings about my book involved not only unreality, but doubt as well. For one thing, it seemed far too long to be a book. More and more frequently, as the piles of manuscript on my desk grew, I would calculate the words I had written (the final draft of *The Power Broker*—not a rough draft, the polished final draft—would be 1,050,000 words, cut to 700,000 words for publication) and I had to wonder if what I was doing would ever be published.

I was bothered, too, by the length not only of the manuscript, but also of the time I had been working on it.

That was the thing that made me doubt the most. When I had started, I had firmly believed that I would be done in a year, a naïve but perhaps not unnatural belief for someone whose longest previous deadline had been measured in weeks. As year followed year, and I was still not nearly done, I became convinced that I had gone terribly astray.

This feeling was fed by the people Ina and I did know. I was still in the first year of research when friends and acquaintances began to ask if I was "still doing that book." Later I would be asked, "How long have you been working on it now?" When I said three years, or four, or five, they would quickly disguise their look of incredulity, but not quickly enough to keep me from seeing it. I came to dread that question.

One day in 1971, I came across a magazine article describing the Frederick Lewis Allen Room. It said that the only requirement for admission was a contract from a publisher, and that its eleven resident writers were allowed to keep books and other research materials at their desks.

The last statement was the one that caught my interest. Users of the Main Reading Room on the library's third floor, where I had done research, were required to return their books every night and to request them again the next morning, a procedure so time-consuming that I had given up on it, and had stopped using the Reading Room entirely. As soon as I read the article, I applied for the Allen Room, and, after a wait of some months, was assigned one of the eleven desks.

Being able to keep material at your desk was wonderful, and so were the materials. There seemed to be no document or report you needed that was not housed somewhere in that great building on Fifth Avenue or in one of its annexes, and that would not appear with seemingly miraculous speed on the cart just inside the Allen Room door after you had looked it up in the card catalogue, written your name and its call number on a pink slip and handed the slip to one of the always helpful librarians upstairs. Moses'

Ph.D. thesis; a volume of "Yale Verse" he had edited in 1909; the city comptroller's confidential reports on the financing of Moses' 1964–65 World's Fair (and on his 1939 World's Fair): the New York Public Library seemed to have, readily at hand, anything I might need on Moses or on the history of New York City.

(And as I would subsequently learn, not just on the history of New York. Years later, working on a biography of Lyndon B. Johnson and living in Texas, I was told there might be a description of one of Johnson's forebears in a three-volume collection of unedited reminiscences by "The Trail Drivers of Texas," published in Dallas in 1929. Ina and I searched for those volumes in libraries and used bookstores all over Texas without success; returning to New York, and checking back into the Allen Room, I decided to look up the collection in the New York Public Library's catalogue. There it was; I filled out a pink slip, and an hour or so later, the three volumes—invaluable volumes, as it turned out—were sitting on the Allen Room cart.)

IT WAS NOT books, however, that were the most wonderful things I found in the Allen Room.

When I had used my key for the first time, opened the big door and, carrying my typewriter, walked into the room, none of the people at the desks in it looked up from their work to give me more than a cursory glance. But one of the glances was from a face easily recognizable because of its patriarchal beard; I recognized it because I had seen it not long before on television. The man sitting at the desk next to me was Joseph P. Lash, author of a book that I much admired, *Eleanor and Franklin*.

And that evening, after everyone in the room had left, I walked from desk to desk reading the names on the pink slips sticking out of the books, to find out the identity of the people sitting there. One of the names was "Milford"—Nancy Milford, who had written *Zelda*. One was "Flexner." The compact little man with the muttonchop whiskers who had been sitting at the first desk when I walked in—who had sat, in shirtsleeves and suspenders, typing diligently hour after hour without even looking up—was James Thomas Flexner, who had already published three volumes of his magisterial biography of George Washington.

Another name was "Lundberg." That was a name that might have faded somewhat from the consciousness of literary America, but it had faded not at all from mine; time and again, when I had been writing about the powerful Gold Coast robber barons who had fought Moses on Long Island, I had turned for facts—always there and always reliable—to *America's 60 Families*, written in 1937 by Ferdinand Lundberg. The day I read the names of the writers to whose work space I had been admitted was the day that I felt I might be a writer, after all.

And these writers provided more for me than merely the glow of their names. In my memory, no one spoke to me for the first few days I was in the room. Then one day, I looked up and James Flexner was standing over me. The expression on his face was friendly, but after he had asked what I was writing about, the next question was the question I had come to dread: "How long have you been working on it?" This time, however, when I replied, "Five years," the response was not an incredulous stare.

"Oh," Jim Flexner said, "that's not so long. I've been working on my Washington for nine years."

I could have jumped up and kissed him, whiskers and all—as, the next day, I could have jumped up and kissed Joe Lash, big beard and all, when he asked me the same question, and, after hearing my answer, said in his quiet way, "*Eleanor and Frank-*

lin took me seven years." In a couple of sentences, these two men—idols of mine—had wiped away five years of doubt.

After a while, the writers of the Allen Room invited me to lunch, which we thereafter ate almost every day in the employees' cafeteria in the library basement. These writers included not just some who were already famous, but some who were, at the time, little better known than I was, like John Demaray, Lucy Komisar, Irene Mahoney and Susan Brownmiller, who was working on *Against Our Will* and would sit at the desk adjoining mine for the next two years, her petite feet, clad in brightly striped socks, sticking under the partition that divided our desks, giving me an odd feeling of companionship.

The cafeteria setting could hardly have been more grubby—or more gratifying. The talk was often about problems of research and writing: about the mysteries of our craft, our shared craft. Suddenly, just by being given a desk in the Allen Room, I had been made to feel a part of the community of writers.

On a row of bookshelves in the Allen Room were copies of the books that had been written there, not merely the Lash, Milford, Flexner, and Lundberg books, but also Betty Friedan's *The Feminine Mystique* and Theodore H. White's *The Making of the President: 1964.*

In September, 1974, *The Power Broker* was published, and I went off on a promotion tour, and then on a long vacation. One day, in the spring of the following year, I waited until the evening, when I knew the room might be empty, and went back to see if *The Power Broker* was on those shelves.

It was.

That was the place, of all places, where it belonged.

The New York Times, May 19, 1995

Lyndon Johnson

W hile I was researching *The Power Broker,* and learning more and more about Robert Moses' amassing
of political power and use of political power, I came
to feel more and more strongly what I had felt when I first conceived of the book: that if (and this was a big "if" with me) I
could just write it well enough, tell the story of his life the way it
should be told, that story would cast light on the realities of urban
political power, power in cities, power not just in New York but
in all the cities of America in the middle of the twentieth century.
And when I finished that book, I knew the one I would like to do
next: a book about national political power. And I felt that I had
learned that if you chose the right man, you could show quite a
bit about power through the life of that man.

But you have to choose the right man. How do you do that?

I spent a lot of time trying to figure that out. I came to feel
that one way was to find someone who had done something no
one had done before, as Robert Moses, in a democracy in which
political power supposedly comes from being elected, had, without ever being elected to anything, amassed an unprecedented
amount of power—far more power, in fact, than any city or state
official who *had* been elected—had held that power for more than
four decades, and with it had done so much to shape a great city
in the image he wanted. If you choose that man, the man who

did something no one else had done, and can figure out how he did it, you get insights into the essence of power.

So I said, Who did something like that nationally? Something that no one had done before. Lyndon Johnson. It was his six years—1955 through 1960—as Senate Majority Leader. For a hundred years before Lyndon Johnson, since the halcyon era of Webster, Clay, and Calhoun, no one had been able to make the Senate work—as, in the fifty-nine years since Lyndon Johnson left the Senate, no one's been able to make the Senate work. But he made it work. During the six years of his leadership, in fact, the Senate became the center of governmental ingenuity, creativity and energy in Washington. For example, no civil rights bill had passed the Senate since 1875, during Reconstruction. In 1957, he succeeded in passing a civil rights bill, a weak one, but a necessary first step toward getting a stronger one—it was the first civil rights bill to pass in eighty-two years. When he set out to pass it, passage seemed impossible in a Senate utterly dominated by the mighty "Southern Caucus." How did he do it? In the Johnson Library, you can see his Senate tally sheets, with the names of the then ninety-six senators. And every day Johnson had a new tally sheet, and you can see the vote changing day by day as he fights for those votes one by one. I wanted to figure out how he changed the votes.

LBJA

When you walk into the Lyndon Baines Johnson Library and Museum for the first time, you are in the building's museum portion, and you see Johnson's long, black, armored presidential limousine and letters he and his mother exchanged while he was in college. I asked the receptionist at the front desk where the Lyndon Johnson Papers were, and she said I would see them if I walked down to the end of the first row of exhibits and turned the corner.

So I did.

In front of me was a broad, tall marble staircase. At its top was a glass wall four stories high. Behind the glass, on each of the four stories, were rows of tall red boxes—175 rows across, each row six boxes high—with, on the front of each box, a gold circle that was a replica, I was to learn, of the presidential seal. All I could see from the bottom of the stairs were those boxes, but as I climbed the stairs, there came into view behind them more boxes, long lines of them. The only light on the four floors was that at the front, and the rows of boxes stretched back into gloom and then darkness as far as I could see.

I took an elevator up to the library's tenth floor to be interviewed by an archivist and given a card admitting me to the Library's Reading Room, where researchers had their desks and could request the boxes that they wanted to look through; the card was good for six months, and would have to be renewed then. The archivist asked me if I thought I would need a renewal. I said probably.

Unfortunately for my peace of mind, I asked if I could be given a look at one of the four floors of boxes, and unfortunately my request was granted. It was like asking a doctor to be honest and give you all the bad news, and having him do just that. I started walking down an aisle between shelves of boxes, six shelves on each side, walls of boxes taller than me. It seemed like a long way to the end of the aisle. And what was looming over me, stretching before me, were just two rows of boxes, of the nine rows on that floor. There were four floors of boxes.

I asked the archivist how many boxes there were, and how many pages of documents each box held. There were about forty thousand boxes, she said; each had a theoretical capacity of eight hundred pages, but of course, she said, not all of them were completely filled, and some were over-filled; if I would like to know the total number of pages in the boxes, she *could* tell me that: thirty-two million. I had known that doing research on a president would be a lot different from doing it on Robert Moses, but I hadn't expected anything like this. I had a bad feeling: during all the years since Alan Hathway had given me that first piece of advice—"Turn every page. Never assume anything. Turn every goddamned page"—I had never forgotten it; it was engraved in my mind. There would be no turning every page here.

BUT WHAT PAGES to turn?

I get a sick feeling in my stomach even now as I remember how long it took to answer that question. I started by looking through the library's "Finding Aids," a version of a catalogue in black looseleaf notebooks that listed the titles of the file folders in each box. Just for Johnson's "House of Representatives Papers," abbreviated by the library as "JHP," the general files from his office during his eleven years in that body, the time before he was senator and president, there were 349 boxes, containing certainly more—perhaps a lot more—than 200,000 pages, and those weren't the only boxes in which there were file folders that contained letters, memoranda, reports, speech drafts, etc., that dealt with this period. There were, for example, the "LBJA" files, which included documents that Johnson's staff had, at various times, shifted from the general "House Papers" files in his office and put into other groupings—the library calls them "collections"—because they were "considered historically valuable or dealt with persons with whom he was closely associated," collections such as the "Congressional File" (LBJA CF), correspondence with fellow congressmen and senators; the "Selected Names" files (LBJA SN), which contained correspondence and other material with "close associates" that had been taken out of the House Papers, etc., etc. There were sixty-one boxes of LBJA material. And there were other collections from the congressional period as well that contained in the neighborhood of forty-eight thousand pages. At least it wouldn't be me alone turning the pages. Working in the Reading Room with me would be Ina, in whose thoroughness and perceptivity in doing research I had learned to trust. There weren't going to be many breaks for lunch: the library was open only from nine to five—on Saturdays only until noon—and that wasn't nearly enough hours, considering what we had to do.

The way things worked: you'd fill out a slip for the boxes—"JHP 167," "LBJA SN 23"—you wanted, and in an hour or so an archivist would arrive in the Reading Room wheeling a cart with the boxes on it, and put them on the cart next to your desk, each of them landing with an impressively, and depressingly, heavy thud. A box would remain there until the day—or the next day, or the next—when you finished looking through the file folders it contained. You'd carry it up to the archivist's desk and give it back. There was room on the cart for only fifteen boxes, and I always had requested more than fifteen, so that when a gap appeared on my cart, it would be so quickly filled with another box that I never had to worry about running out of material.

OBVIOUSLY WE COULDN'T turn every page, or even a substantial percentage of them. But I knew we had to turn as many as possible. And we turned quite a few, requesting a lot of boxes, looking through a lot of file folders that, from their description in the Finding Aids, one would assume contained nothing of use to me—and the wisdom of Alan's advice was proven to me again and again. Someday, I hope to leave behind me a record of at least a few of the scores and scores of times that that happened, some of which may be of interest, at any rate to fellow historians; for now, I'll give just one example.

I had decided that among the boxes in which I would at least glance at every piece of paper would be the ones in Johnson's general "House Papers" that contained the files from his first years in Congress, since I wanted to be able to paint a picture of what he had been like as a young congressman. I thought that by doing that I could also give some insight into the life of junior congressmen in general. And as I was doing this—reading or at least glancing at every letter and memo, turning every page—I began to get a feeling: something in those early years had changed. For some time after his arrival in Congress, following a special election, in May, 1937, his letters to committee chairmen, to senior congressmen in general, had been in a tone befitting a new congressman with no seniority or power, in the tone of a junior addressing a senior, beseeching a favor, or asking, perhaps, for a few minutes of his time to discuss something. But there were also letters and memos in the same boxes from senior congressmen in which *they* were doing the beseeching, asking for a few minutes of *his* time. What was the reason for the change? Was there a particular time at which it had occurred?

Going back over my notes for all the documents, I put them into chronological order, and when I did it was easy to see that there had indeed been such a time: a single month, October, 1940. Before that month, Lyndon Johnson had been invariably, in his correspondence, the junior to the senior. After that month, and, it became clearer and clearer as I put more and more documents into date order, after a single date—November 5, 1940; Election Day, 1940—the tone was frequently the opposite. And, in fact, after that date, Johnson's files also contained letters written to him by middle-level congressmen, and by other congressmen as junior as he, in a supplicating tone, whereas there had been no such letters—not a single one that I could find—before that date. Obviously the change had had something to do with the election. But what?

At that time, I was constantly flying back and forth between Austin and Washington. Papers don't die; people do, so I was giving first priority, whenever they would give me an appointment, to interviewing the men and women who during the 1930s, forty years before, had been members of a circle of young New Deal insiders to which the young congressman from Texas had been admitted.

One of this circle was Thomas G. Corcoran, the pixieish,

ebullient, accordion-playing Irishman known as "Tommy the Cork," who had been an aide to Franklin Roosevelt, and had since become a legend in Washington as a political fixer and fund-raiser nonpareil. I just loved interviewing Tommy the Cork. He was at that time in his late seventies, but if, on a morning on which I had an appointment with him in his office on the seventh floor of a K Street office building, he came into the lobby while I was waiting for the elevator, he would say, "See you upstairs, kid" as he opened the door to the stairwell, and often, when I reached the seventh floor, he would be standing grinning at me when the elevator door opened. And he was, in the best sense of the word (truly the best to an interviewer anxious to learn the innermost secrets of political maneuverings), totally amoral. He cared for nothing. Once, on a morning on which we had an interview scheduled, I picked up *The Washington Post* over breakfast in my hotel room to see his name in big headlines and read a huge story about his role in a truly sordid Washington scandal. I expected to find a broken, or at least dejected, man when I was ushered into his office. Instead he gave me a big grin—he had the most infectious grin—and, when I didn't bring up the subject of the story but he could tell it was on my mind, said: "It's just free advertising, kid, free advertising. Just as long as they spell my name right." He had once told me one of his most effective fund-raising techniques. When the man he was asking for money wrote a check and handed it across the desk to him, Mr. Corcoran, no matter what the amount—no matter if it was more than he had hoped for—would look at it with an expression of disdain, drop it back on the man's desk, and, without saying a word, walk toward the door. He had never once, he told me—exaggerating, I'm sure, but how much?—he had never once been allowed to reach the door without the man calling him back, tearing up the check, and writing one for a larger amount. And now, when I asked the Cork what had changed Lyndon Johnson's status in October, 1940, he said: "Money, kid, money." Then he added: "But you're never going to be able to write about that." I asked why not. "Because you're never going to find anything in writing," he said.

FOR SOME TIME, I was afraid Mr. Corcoran was right. From what I had already learned about Johnson's obsession with secrecy, I was quite prepared to believe that in this particularly sensitive area he had made sure that there was going to be nothing to find. And the Cork was right on another point, too: without something in writing—documentation, in other words—about this most sensitive of political areas, even if I discovered what had happened, I wasn't going to be able to put it in my book. But the change in Johnson's status—the fact that October, 1940, was a turning point in his career, that during that month this young congressman had been elevated above the ranks of other young congressmen to a place of some significance in the House of Representatives—made me feel it was imperative that I find out and document what had happened in that month. What had made so many congressmen—including powerful senior congressmen, barons of Capitol Hill—become supplicants to him, asking this junior congressman for a few minutes of his time? And if indeed the transformation had to do with money, I had to find documentation of what had happened; without something in writing, *I* wasn't going to be able to write about it.

But Alan's words were in my mind. I had been looking at only Lyndon Johnson's general "House Papers" because I knew they bore on an area—Lyndon Johnson as a young congressman—that

I was planning to include in my book. But the boxes labeled "House Papers" might not be the only boxes that dealt with Johnson's early congressional career. There were also, for example, those LBJA files. I hadn't even begun turning the pages in them.

I started to rethink things. Among the boxes of documents that had been taken out of Johnson's general "House Papers" and put into other "collections" including the "Selected Names" collection, were the LBJA boxes, the collection of letters and memos to and from "close associates." And Corcoran had said the answer to my question was "money," and if money was involved, the place to start looking was at Brown & Root, the Texas road- and dam-building firm whose principals, Herman and George Brown (Root had died years before), had been before 1940 the secret but major financiers of Johnson's early career and had already, before 1940, begun receiving federal contracts through his efforts. When it came to money, there were no closer associates than Herman and George. I didn't have much hope of finding anything in writing, but their files were files in which I should nonetheless have been turning every page.

I started doing that now. To make room on my cart, I lugged up to the archivist's desk a number of general "House Papers" boxes and requested boxes from the "Selected Names" collection instead. When they arrived, I started with Box 13 and pulled out the file folders for Herman. A lot of fascinating material in their 237 pages which I could use later in my books, but nothing shedding light on the 1940 change in which I was interested. George's correspondence was in Box 12. There were about 230 pages in his file. I sat there turning the pages, every page, thinking that I was probably just wasting more days of my life. And then, suddenly, as I lifted yet another innocuous letter to put it aside, the next document was not a letter but a Western Union telegram form, turned brown during the decades since it had been sent—on October 19, 1940. It was addressed to Lyndon Johnson, and was signed "George Brown," and it said, in the capital letters Western Union used for its messages: YOU WERE SUPPOSED TO HAVE CHECKS BY FRIDAY . . . HOPE THEY ARRIVED IN DUE FORM AND ON TIME. It also named the people who were supposed to have sent the checks: six of Brown & Root's subcontractors. And Tommy Corcoran had been wrong: Lyndon Johnson *had* put something in writing. Attached to the telegram was a copy of his response to George. ALL OF THE FOLKS YOU TALKED TO HAVE BEEN HEARD FROM, it said. I AM NOT ACKNOWLEDGING THEIR LETTERS, SO BE SURE TO TELL ALL THESE FELLOWS THAT THEIR LETTERS HAVE BEEN RECEIVED . . . YOUR FRIEND, LYNDON B. JOHNSON. Johnson had added by hand: "The thing is exceeding my expectations. The Boss is listening to my suggestions, thanks to your encouragements [*sic*]."

So there was the proof that Lyndon Johnson had received money from Brown & Root in October, 1940 (and that it had brought him into some sort of contact with "The Boss," Johnson's name for President Franklin Roosevelt). In his telegram, Brown named six people who were supposed to have sent the checks. How much had they sent? What scale of money were we talking about? Why hadn't Brown & Root sent the money itself? And more important, what had happened to the money? How did Johnson use it? How was it distributed? What was the mechanism by which it was distributed? There was no clue in the telegram, or in Johnson's reply. But the money had come from Texas, and George and Herman had friends who, I knew, had been contributing, at the Browns' insistence, to Johnson's first campaigns. Most of the contributors, I had been told, were oilmen, in Texas parlance "big oilmen." I started calling for the big oilmen's folders in LBJA SN. And, sure enough, there was a letter, dated in October, from one of the biggest of the oilmen, Clint Murchison.

Murchison dealt with senators or with the Speaker of the House, Sam Rayburn; he hardly knew the young congressman; in his letter to Johnson, he misspelled his name as "Linden." But he was evidently following Brown & Root's lead. "We are enclosing herewith the check of the Aloco Oil Co. for $5,000, payable to the Democratic Congressional Committee," his letter said. Another big oilman was Charles F. Roeser of Fort Worth: the amount mentioned in the letter I found from him was again five thousand, the payee the same.

So the entity was the Democratic Congressional Committee, or, to give it its full title, the Democratic Congressional Campaign Committee, which had previously been nothing more than a moribund subsidiary of the Democratic National Committee. There were a lot of file folders in Boxes 6 and 7 of the Johnson House Papers labeled: "Democratic National Committee." Those boxes were crammed to capacity. Some of the folders had less than inviting titles: "General—Unarranged," for example. That was a thick folder, bulging with papers that had been sloppily crammed into it. When I pulled it out of its box, I remember asking myself if I really had to do "General—Unarranged." But Alan might possibly have been proud of me—and I wasn't very deep into the folder when I was certainly grateful to him. One of the six people in George Brown's telegram whom Brown said had sent checks was named "Corwin." In "General—Unarranged," not in alphabetical order but just jammed in, was a note from J. O. Corwin, a Brown & Root subcontractor, saying he was "enclosing herewith my check for $5,000, payable to the Democratic Congressional Campaign Committee." Five thousand dollars. Had each of the six men mentioned in Brown's letter sent that amount? That seemed likely, and if they had, then that would have been thirty thousand dollars—a substantial amount in the politics of that era. The "Unarranged" file contained, not of course in alphabetical order, letter after letter with details I knew I could use. In other folders, also, were letters in which that same amount was mentioned: five thousand from E. S. Fentress, who I knew had been the partner of Johnson's patron, Charles Marsh. Were all the donations from Texas in that amount? Big oilmen! One of the biggest, and most politically astute, was Sid Richardson. I looked under the name "Richardson" in file folder after file folder in different collections without any luck. What was the name of that nephew of his whom Richardson, unmarried and childless, allowed to transact some of his business affairs? I had heard it somewhere. What *was* it? Bass, Perry Bass. I found that name and the donation: "Perry R. Bass, $5,000" in yet another box in the House papers. Letters from many big Texas oilmen of the 1940s—the oilmen who needed guarantees that the oil depletion allowance wouldn't be taken away, that other, more arcane, tax breaks conferred by the federal government, wouldn't be touched—were scattered through those boxes. And all the contributions were for five thousand dollars. Of course, they *must be.* My mind was into all the things I had been reading about political financing and I suddenly remembered what I should have remembered before. Under federal law in 1940 the limit on an individual contribution was five thousand dollars. How could I have been so slow to get it? Well, I got it now. The Brown & Root contribution to the Democratic Congressional

Campaign Committee, funneled through the company's business associates, had been thirty thousand dollars, more money than the Committee had received from its parent National Committee. And there were so many additional five-thousand-dollar contributions from Texas!

BUT THERE WAS a next question: how had this money resulted in such a great change in Lyndon Johnson's status in Congress? How had he transmuted those contributions into power for himself? He had had no title or formal position with the Democratic Congressional Campaign Committee; he had tried to get one, I had learned from other files, but had been rebuffed.

I found the answer in those LBJA files. He had had George Brown instruct each of the "Brown & Root" contributors, and had had the other Texas contributors instructed similarly, to enclose with their checks a letter stating: "I would like for this money to be expended in connection with the campaign of Democratic candidates for Congress as per the list attached." Johnson had, of course, compiled the list, and while the checks received by the lucky candidates might have been issued by the Democratic Congressional Campaign Committee, each candidate received a telegram from Johnson saying the check had been sent AS RESULT MY VISIT TO CONGRESSIONAL COMMITTEE FEW MINUTES AGO.

BEFORE THE CAMPAIGN was over—in that single month, October, 1940—Lyndon Johnson had raised from Texas and had distributed to congressional candidates, campaign funds on a scale that dwarfed anything ever given to Democratic congressional candidates from a single, central source. The documents in those boxes of Johnson "House of Representatives Papers" made that clear. And as I turned the pages in those boxes there were other documents. "General—Unarranged" contained another list. There were two typed columns on each of its thirteen pages, typed by either John Connally or Walter Jenkins; each of these Johnson assistants was to tell me that he had been the one who had typed it. In the left-hand column were the districts of congressmen who had asked the Congressional Committee for money. In the second column were the names of the congressmen and the amount each had asked for—tiny amounts in the terms of later eras—and what, in the congressman's own telegraphed words, he needed it for. MUST HAVE $250 BY THURSDAY NIGHT FOR LAST ISSUE ADVERTISING, for example. Or $350 BY THURSDAY. HAVE SET UP MACHINERY TO REACH 11,000 ADDITIONAL VOTERS BY MAIL. Or COULD USE $500 FOR WORKERS IN SPANISH AND ITALIAN DISTRICTS. Or NEED $1,000 NOVEMBER 1ST TO HIRE POLL WATCHERS. Or CHANCES BRIGHT . . . IF WE CAN GET RIGHT AWAY $14 FOR EACH OF FIVE COUNTY PAPERS AND $20 FOR TITUSVILLE HERALD.

And there was also a third column on the page, or, rather, handwritten notations in the left-hand margin, next to each district, notes dealing with each congressman's request. The handwriting in that column was Lyndon Johnson's. If he was arranging for the candidate to be given part or all of what he had asked for, Johnson wrote, "OK—$500" or "OK—$200" or whatever the amount he had decided to give. If he did not want the candidate to be given anything, he wrote "None." And, by some names, he wrote: "None—Out." (What did "None—Out" mean?, I was later to ask John Connally. "It meant he [the candidate] was *never* going to get *anything*," Connally said. "Lyndon Johnson never forgot, and he never forgave.")

Lyndon Johnson had identified a source of financing for congressional races across the United States, a source that had in the past been used principally on behalf of presidential or senatorial candidates, senatorial candidates mostly from Texas: Texas money. Using the power of House Speaker Sam Rayburn of Texas, he had made sure the money came only through him. When, in 1940, officials of the Democratic Congressional Campaign Committee had attempted to go around him directly to the source, writing directly to the oilmen to request contributions, the oilmen had asked Rayburn whom to send the money to, and the oilman had thereupon replied not to the committee but to Lyndon Johnson, writing, in the words of one of them, Charles Roeser, I HAVE DECIDED TO SEND MY CONTRIBUTION . . . TO YOU. . . . I AM . . . LEAVING IT UP TO . . . YOU, TO DECIDE IN WHAT DISTRICTS THESE FUNDS CAN BE BEST USED. And Johnson was not only deciding which candidates would get the money, he was making sure the candidates knew they were getting it from *him*. "I want to see you win," he said to them in his letters and telegrams. And here is some money to help. After I finished going through those boxes, I was able to write: "A new source of political money, potentially vast, had been tapped in America, and Lyndon Johnson had been put in charge of it." And, by the time the congressmen got back to Washington in November after the elections and talked to one another, the word was out. "There was a lot of gratitude for what he had done," Walter Jenkins said. "He was *the* hero."

Moreover, the congressmen were going to need money for future campaigns, and they had learned that a good way to get it—in some cases the only way—was through Lyndon Johnson. They were going to need *him*. "Gratitude," I was to write, "is an emotion as ephemeral in Washington as elsewhere but . . . not merely gratitude but an emotion perhaps somewhat stronger and more enduring—self-interest—dictated that they be on good terms with him." As one congressman from that era told me: after October, 1940, "We knew . . . he had already started going somewhere. . . . He was a guy you couldn't deny anymore." In that single month, Lyndon Johnson, thirty-two years old, just three years in the House, had established himself as a congressman with a degree of power over other congressmen, as a congressman who had gained his first toehold on the national power he was to wield for the next thirty years. For someone interested in the sources of political power, as I was, those boxes in the Johnson Library contained such clear evidence of the use to which economic power could be put to create political power.

TO MY WAY of thinking, I had only one question left, and there was only one man who could answer it. I might know the answer, but knowing it wasn't proving it. Herman Brown was dead. I had to talk to George.

I had known that wasn't going to be easy. George and Herman had been proud of their attitude toward would-be interviewers; they had often boasted, with some exaggeration, that neither of them had ever given an interview, and that neither of them ever would. Herman had died before I started on my Johnson books, and George was apparently going to honor the brotherly code. I had been trying to talk to him ever since I started on Lyndon Johnson, with no results, or indeed response. When I telephoned and left a message with his secretary he never called back; when I wrote him letters there was no reply. After I became friends with Brown & Root's longtime chief lobbyist, Frank "Posh" Oltorf, I asked Posh to intercede, and he did, several times—after which he told me quite firmly that Mr. Brown was never going to talk to me. And if he didn't, I was going to have a hard time proving in my book *why* Brown & Root had given the money—or, indeed, why over the decades after 1940, they had given Lyndon Johnson such an immense amount of financial backing.

Sometimes, a sudden thought does the job. One day, I found myself, in my endless driving around the Hill Country, in the little town of Burnet. In the courthouse square, among the weathered wooden storefronts, there was a handsome new building with the legend "Herman Brown Free Library" on it.

All at once, something occurred to me. George had loved and idolized his older brother, who had really been more like a father to him than a brother. Since Herman's death, George had been building public monuments to him all over Texas, not only Herman Brown public libraries, but a Herman Brown Hall for Mathematical Sciences at Rice University. There was a telephone booth in the Burnet square. From it I telephoned Posh, and asked him to call George one more time. Posh said quite firmly that he wasn't going to do that. I'm only asking you to call one more time, I said, and I want you to say just one sentence to him: tell him that no matter how many buildings he puts Herman Brown's name on, in a few years no one is going to know who Herman Brown *was* if he's not in a book.

I don't remember Posh's reply, but he evidently made the call. The next morning, very early, before I was awake, the phone rang, and it was Mr. Brown's secretary, asking what time would be convenient for me to meet with him.

I THOUGHT WE GOT along very well. When I was ushered in to his office, I found myself with a seventy-nine-year-old man who was almost blind but still vigorous and clear of mind. After he and Herman had begun in the 1930s to build the Marshall Ford Dam, the biggest project on which Brown & Root had ever embarked, and had sunk a million and a half dollars of the firm's money into it, they found that, because of a quirk in the law, the dam was, in Brown's words, "illegal," and therefore that any federal appropriation for it would be illegal. "We had already built the cableway. That cost hundreds of thousands of dollars, which we owed the banks. . . . We had put in a million and a half dollars," he explained to me. The federal government had been supposed to appropriate the money for it in its 1937 session, but it had now been discovered that any appropriation wouldn't be legal. The Browns were facing bankruptcy. Johnson, new to Congress though he was, had worked out a device to make it legal. And the Browns had been grateful. ("Remember that I am *for* you, right or wrong, and it makes no difference if I think you are right or wrong. If you want it, I am for it, 100%," George wrote him, in another letter I found in LBJA SN.) And Johnson had done more for the Browns, had seen to it that they received the biggest contract they had ever received: to build the Corpus Christi Naval Air Station ("Johnson got us into Corpus Christi," George told me flatly) and then had seen that they were given more contracts—contracts that totaled hundreds of millions of dollars—to build subchasers and destroyers for the Navy, although, as Mr. Brown told me, "We didn't know the stern from the aft—I mean the bow—of the boat." At the end of our interview, which lasted an entire day, he said he had enjoyed it, and would I like to come again. I said I would, and we went to lunch at the Riata Club. Afterwards, he took me to see the legendary "8-F," Suite 8-F at Houston's Lamar Hotel, where the biggest of Texas's big oilmen and contractors met to map out the state's political future. But evidently the friendliness wasn't as deep as I thought. When my book, *The Path to Power*, came out, and Johnson's associates and the Johnson Library were busy attacking it, George Brown told the library that I had misquoted him.

"Why Can't You Do a Biography of Napoleon?"

Ina and I would spend all day reading documents in the John-son Library, I at one desk, Ina at another a few desks away. And then at a quarter to five the archivist would announce that the Reading Room was about to close and I'd take the elevator downstairs, walk out of the museum past the exhibits showing Lyndon Johnson as President, get into my car and drive out to the Hill Country, to find out what Lyndon Johnson had been like as a boy and young man.

Johnson died at sixty-four. At the time I started these books, he would have been only sixty-seven. So most of the people who went to high school or college with him were still alive, and, in fact, still living in or around Johnson City. If Truman Fawcett, one of his best friends in high school, had lived back then on the other side of the courthouse square, well, Truman Fawcett was still living on the other side of the courthouse square. Kitty Clyde Ross, Lyndon Johnson's first girlfriend (until her parents made her stop seeing him because he was "a Johnson") was Kitty Clyde Leonard now, but she was still in Johnson City, available to be talked to (and asked what it had been like to take the ride on Air Force One that Lyndon had given her when he became President).

I had thought I would only have to write a chapter or two on

Johnson's youth, and wouldn't have to do much research for it. At the time I started there were already seven biographies of Johnson in print, all of them with a chapter or two on that period of his life. And they all related the same anecdotes, which portrayed young Lyndon as a sort of Horatio Alger hero of the Hill Country, smiling and popular, who had risen through ambition and hard work. Wonderful anecdotes, some of them. Poor boy making his way in the world. I thought that thanks to those books I already knew the basic story of his youth, without enough detail or sense of what the Hill Country was like, but that I could provide through some interviews and that was all I would need to do.

I found the interviews unexpectedly difficult, however—very difficult, in fact. Some of the people who had known Lyndon in college lived on isolated ranches or farms. I would drive sixty or seventy miles on a highway and then ("Look for the cattle guard on the left"), turn off onto an unpaved track that might go for fifteen or twenty miles, and at the end of it would be a house, the only one for miles, and in it a couple (or a widow; there seemed to be a disproportionate number of widows in the Hill Country) who weren't accustomed to having long conversations with strangers. And the barrier was not simply a shyness which I could break down. The ranchers and farmers of the Hill Country were very different from people in New York. There was a kind of reticence, of holding back, in their conversations with me, a laconic quality which didn't provide much information. Moreover, they also felt—quite deeply, in a trait especially striking to someone from New York and particularly to someone from New York's Upper West Side—that it was wrong to say anything derogatory about a man who had become President of the United States. While if you asked them a direct question, they would always tell you the truth, they wouldn't volunteer anything; their answers would be terse, brief. I got the feeling that what they were telling me was only part of the story of the young Lyndon Johnson. I'd repeat one of those wonderful anecdotes that were in the other biographies, and the most someone might volunteer was, "Well, that's not quite what happened." They wouldn't say what actually *had* happened, and were very chary about giving me any details. I began to sense a deep reluctance to tell me the whole story, or even the true story—to reveal to an outsider what Lyndon Johnson had really been like as a youth and young man. Equally disturbing, the more I talked to them, the more I realized that it wasn't just the young Lyndon Johnson I wasn't understanding, the same was true of the people to whom I was talking: I wasn't understanding them, either—their culture, their mores. They were obviously very different from me, or from any people I had encountered before, and I didn't know how to break through.

Part of the problem, I came to realize, was that they had talked to too many people like me. During Lyndon Johnson's presidency, journalists from all over the United States, from every major magazine and newspaper and a lot of minor ones, too, had come to the Hill Country, had spent three or four days there (or even a week), and had gone home to explain this remote place to the rest of America. Hill Country people had a name for them: "portable journalists." They basically thought I was a portable journalist too.

I said to Ina, "I'm not understanding these people and therefore I'm not understanding Lyndon Johnson. We're going to have to move to the Hill Country and live there." Ina said, "Why can't you do a biography of Napoleon?" But Ina is always Ina: loyal and true. She said, as she always says: "Sure." We rented a house on the edge of the Hill Country, where we were to live for most of the next three years.

That changed everything. As soon as we had moved there, as soon as the people of the Hill Country realized we were there to stay, their attitude towards us softened; they started to talk to me in a different way. I began to hear the details they had not included in the anecdotes they had previously told me—and they told me other anecdotes and longer stories, anecdotes and stories that no one had even mentioned to me before—stories about a Lyndon Johnson very different from the young man who had previously been portrayed: stories about a very unusual young man, a very brilliant young man, a very ambitious, unscrupulous and quite ruthless person, disliked and even despised, and, by people who knew him especially well, even beginning to be feared.

ONE THING THAT LIVING in the Hill Country did for me was to get to know Lyndon's little brother, Sam Houston Johnson.

I had, of course, interviewed Sam Houston several times already, while we were still living in Austin. He had a reputation not only for a severe drinking problem but for bravado, braggadocio, for exaggeration that bordered on untruthfulness, and I had found the reputation fully justified. It didn't ameliorate my feelings for him that he played the archetypal Texan: big hat, big boots, a bottle of Tabasco sauce that he always carried in his pocket because food was never spicy enough for him; and, I felt, big—tall—stories. He told me the same stories about Lyndon that others had, but with fanciful details added, all to glorify his brother, but it seemed to me that every actual fact in his anecdotes that could be checked would, when I checked it, turn out to be either exaggerated or entirely false. Feeling I had wasted enough time checking, I had decided to simply not use anything he told me.

I didn't see Sam Houston for perhaps a year.

During this interval, I heard that he had had a horrible operation for cancer, that he had to use a cane all the time now, and that he had stopped drinking. Then, one day, while I was walking around the streets of Johnson City—I was there a lot, just chatting with people, trying to absorb the atmosphere; walking the sidewalks, a few paved, some wooden, some just dust; saying, "Howdy" to everyone I met; trying to remember that the noun was not "you" but "y'all"—there he was, limping toward me, shrunken, frail. We went to have a cup of coffee in Casparis' Café (you venture too far beyond coffee in that café at your peril; Lady Bird Johnson told me once, in a rare moment of acerbity, that when forced to eat there she always ordered eggs: "There isn't too much they can do to eggs"). I found the man sitting next to me at the counter now a changed man—quiet, calm, all the braggadocio gone. I decided to try interviewing him again.

There was one thing in particular about which I not only wanted but needed his help, and I had thought of a way I might get it. By this time, having interviewed not only Lyndon Johnson's sister Rebekah, but three cleaning women who had, at one time or another, worked in the Johnson home, I felt that a key to Lyndon Johnson's youth—to his character throughout his life, in fact, the character that had had such a profound impact on American history—was his complicated relationship with his father, Sam Ealy Johnson, whom he so strikingly resembled, not only in appearance but in manner. It was a relationship that veered from idolization to hatred, but I didn't have a clear picture of that relationship in my mind, and not enough detail to make my readers see it. Here was someone who had seen it every day, including every evening when Lyndon and his father sat down with the family for dinner. And I had thought of a device that I hoped might elicit from Sam Houston the true picture of that relationship—the details of it—that I needed; that might put him back, in his mind, into his childhood, that might make his memory of the relationship become as clear to him as possible.

I persuaded the National Park Service to allow Sam Houston and me to go into the Johnson Boyhood Home in Johnson City, which had been faithfully re-created to look as it had when Lyndon was growing up in it, after it had officially closed for the day. And one evening, when it was empty, with the tourists and guides all gone, I took Sam Houston Johnson into the house in which he had been a boy.

I led him into the dining room. There was a long plank table, just like the one around which the Johnsons had gathered for meals. At its head and foot were high-backed chairs, for the father and mother. When the Johnsons had dined there, Rebekah and her two sisters had sat side by side in chairs on one side of the table, and Lyndon and Sam Houston had sat on the other.

I asked Sam Houston to sit in the same place he had sat in as a boy. Despite his lameness, he threw a leg over one of the chairs, put his cane down next to it, and, pulling over his other leg, sat down, next to his father's old chair, as if he were a boy sitting there again.

I didn't sit down at the table. I sat down instead behind Sam Houston, in a chair against the wall, and it was sitting there that I opened my notebook. I didn't want anyone at that table who was not one of the Johnsons of Johnson City.

It was about the same time of day that would have been dinnertime in Johnson City long ago. Rays of the low evening sun came into the dining room and cast shadows, the same shadows the sun would have cast as Sam Houston had sat there as a boy.

"Now, Sam Houston," I said. "I'd like you to tell me again about those terrible arguments that your father and Lyndon used to have at dinnertime—just take me through them again, like you did before, only with more detail."

At first, it was slow going, halting, just fragments of generalized memory, and I had to keep interjecting myself to keep it going at all: "Daddy would say something about . . ." *And then what?* "Well, Lyndon would say . . ." But once Sam Houston started remembering, the memories, strikingly different from others he had previously given, began coming clearer and faster until finally no interjections were necessary, and there were no pauses: Sam Houston was re-creating family dinners at the Johnsons', saying, almost shouting, back and forth, what his father had shouted at his brother, and what his brother had shouted back: "You're just not college material, are you, goddammit? You're just a failure, Lyndon, and you're always going to be a failure . . ." and Lyndon would shout back, "What are *you?* You're a bus inspector, that's what you are! . . ." " 'Sam!, Sam!,' Mother would say . . . 'Lyndon!, Lyndon!' "

Sitting there against the wall, I felt I was getting closer to the heart of Lyndon Johnson's boyhood. And when, finally, after quite a long time, Sam Houston had stopped talking, and was sitting quietly, very quiet and still, so still that I felt he was in the grip of memory, memory as true as it could be after all these years, I said to him: "Now, Sam Houston, I want you to tell me again all those wonderful stories about Lyndon when you both were boys, the stories you told me before—just tell me them again with more details."

There was a long pause. I can still see the scene—see the little, stunted, crippled man sitting at the long plank table, see the shadows in the room, see myself, not wanting to move lest I break the spell, sitting there with my notebook against the wall saying, "Tell me those wonderful stories again."

"I can't," Sam Houston said.

"Why not?" I asked.

"Because they never happened."

I don't think there was a pause after that. In my memory, without a pause from Sam Houston or a question from me, he simply started talking—my notes tell me he began by saying, "No one really understood what happened when Lyndon went to California"—and related, incident after incident, anecdotes from Lyndon Johnson's youth, some of which I had heard before, in shorter, incomplete, and softened versions but which I heard in new, more complete versions now; others that had never been mentioned to me, or, I felt, to anyone else. The shadows lengthened, the room grew darker. The voice went on. By the time, a long time later, that it stopped, I had a different picture of Lyndon Johnson's youth—that terrible youth, that character-hardening youth—than I, or history, had had before. And now, when I went back to the men and women who had been involved in the incidents, and, armed with the details Sam Houston had given me, asked again about these incidents, I got a different response than I had gotten before. Yes, that's what happened, they would say. And, often they would say, there's something else I remember. More details would come. The story at last would be coherent—and closer to the truth.

Interviewing

"I lied under oath":
Luis Salas

I've done so many interviews for my books—522 I see I counted for *The Power Broker*, when I was still counting; for the Johnson books I didn't count: thousands, I guess.

Some of them stick out in your memory, like one with a man named Luis Salas.

A crucial moment in Lyndon Johnson's career was the 1948 election for a United States senator from Texas, which Johnson apparently had lost to former governor Coke Stevenson until, six days after the balloting, Precinct 13—"Box 13"—in Jim Wells County, one of the border counties ruled by Duval County's George Parr, the notorious "Duke of Duval," suddenly reported 202 new votes, 200 of them for Johnson, votes which gave him the victory by eighty-seven votes out of almost a million that had been cast. Every Johnson biography had included some pages on the election, and on the ensuing controversy over whether he had stolen it, but all had treated it somewhat offhandedly and had made some version of the statement: no one will ever know if it was really stolen. Most of these books treated the election as sort of a Texas-size joke, with stealing by both sides.

I remember thinking when I reached 1948 in my research that that election wasn't a topic that I was going to treat offhandedly. Part of the reason was straightforward and professional: what I was trying to do with my books. I was supposed to be examining the political system in America, and there had been a lot of stolen elections in American political history; it wouldn't be exaggerating much, in fact, to say that the stealing of elections was an integral part of that history; I wanted to examine, to dissect, a stolen election in detail. But part of the reason was neither straightforward nor professional, nor, to be honest (or as honest as possible), was it something that had much to do with reason. It had to do with that something in me, that something in my nature, which, as I said earlier, wasn't a quality I could be proud of or could take credit for. It wasn't something that, as I missed yet another deadline by months or years, I could take the blame for, either. It was just part of me, like it or not; the part of me that had hated writing an article for *Newsday* while I still had questions—or even *a* question—left to ask; the part of me that, now that I was writing books, kept leading me, after I had gotten every question answered, to suddenly think, despite myself, of new questions that, in the instant of thinking them, I felt must be answered for my book to be complete; the part of me that kept leading me to think of new avenues of research that, even as I thought of them, I felt it was crucial to head down. It wasn't something about which, I had learned the hard way, I had a choice; in reality I had no choice at all. In my defense: while I am aware that there is no Truth, no objective truth, no single truth, no truth simple or unsimple, either; no verity, eternal or otherwise; no Truth about anything, there *are* Facts, objective facts, discernible and verifiable. And the more facts you accumulate, the closer you come to whatever truth there is. And finding facts—through reading documents or through interviewing and re-interviewing—can't be rushed; it takes time. Truth takes time. But that's a logical way of justifying that quality in me. And I know it wasn't only logic that made me think: I'm never going to write about a crucial election, a pivotal moment in my subject's life, and say that no one's ever going to know if it was really stolen or not until I've done everything I can think of to find out if it was stolen or not.

And that led me to Luis Salas.

I had heard about Salas during my trips to the Rio Grande Valley to learn about George Parr because Salas had been Parr's enforcer, a thickset six-foot-one-inch native of Durango, Mexico, who had, years before, left Mexico in a hurry after killing a man in a barroom brawl. Known as the "Indio" because of his swarthy appearance, he carried a revolver with a barrel so long that when it was in his holster, it reached almost to his knee, and he was known for his fierce temper and for his brutality toward anyone who opposed the Duke; once, when the owner of a restaurant in Alice trying to remain independent in politics dared to start fighting with Salas, his wife screamed, "Stop! Don't you know who you are fighting? He is the man they call the 'Indio.'" After beating the man into unconsciousness, Salas picked up a barstool and wrecked the restaurant. And as presiding election judge at Box 13 during the 1948 election, he had been the key witness, and was actually on the stand, testifying, at the moment that the federal court investigation into the election was abruptly cut short, never to be resumed, by an order from a United States Supreme Court Justice in Washington. If he was alive, I was not going to write about the 1948 election until I had talked to him.

I DROVE DOWN to the Valley again, and in Alice and other towns went into the cafés where elderly men who had been born in Mexico sat chatting in Spanish around tables, and eventually learned that Salas was alive, but had moved to Mexico some years—or decades—before. No one seemed to know to where, however. "Luis moves around a lot," someone said.

I get asked why it takes me so long to produce my books. Let me tell you that trying to track down someone who has left the United States years before and returned to someone where he "moves around a lot" is not a matter of hours. But eventually, in March, 1986, I found him. He was no longer in Mexico; he had come back to Texas—to Houston—where he was living in a mobile home in the spacious tree-shaded backyard of his daughter, Grace, and her family.

When Salas answered my knock, I got quite a shock. Although intellectually, of course, I knew that almost forty years had passed since the 1948 election, I had in my mind the picture of the man as he had looked in 1948 photographs, and I guess was expecting to be looking up—at George Parr's tall, broad, fearsome "Indio." Instead, I found myself looking down—at a stooped, thin, gray-haired old man wearing eyeglasses. And when eighty-four-year-old Luis Salas showed me into the nicely furnished mobile home, his manner was gentle. In the next room, his wife, Tana, sat in a rocking chair, not speaking at all, wrapped in a blanket; several times, as we talked, he got up to wrap it around her more warmly.

And that was not the only shock I received. It took no prompting to persuade Salas, whose eyes behind the glasses were keen and who was quite clear-witted, to talk about the 1948 election, and he confirmed many of the surmises that had been hinted at for decades about what had happened at Box 13. His job had been to pull the ballots—paper ballots—out of the ballot box and call out the name written on them to the other election judges, who were tabulating the vote, and he told me, not at all regretful but grinning, pleased with himself: "If they were not for Johnson, I make them for Johnson." In case I had missed the point, he returned to it a few minutes later, saying, "Any vote for Stevenson I counted for Johnson." A key point in the investigation in the federal court was whether or not Salas had, on election night, reported Johnson's total in the box as 765 to a journalist named Cliff Dubose, and then, six days after the election, had added the 200 additional votes to Johnson's total when he was reporting the results to the Texas Election Commission. Johnson's opponents charged that the number that had been tabulated on election night, the number obtained by Salas having made them for Johnson, whether or not that was what the voter had intended, had been later raised from 765 to 965 by simply adding a loop to the 7 to change it into a 9. Salas had denied under oath that he had ever given the 765 number to Dubose. Now I asked him if he had, in fact, done that. Yes, he said, he had: on election night "I told Cliff 765." But then, as I continued asking questions, he said, "I have written it all down." He stood up and walked over to a trunk. Bending over stiffly, he opened it and pulled out a manuscript. It was a book he had written, ninety-four pages long. Its title was "Box 13."

While we continued talking, I leafed through it. I was caught by a paragraph near the beginning: "Reader, I don't know if my story is to your liking, writing nonfiction is hard, I had no schooling, please excuse my spelling and grammar, but I had to write this book, to leave it to my family, when I go beyond, my time is running short, and I want to finish without adding or subtracting parts that are false, or invented by my imagination, no, everything has to be exactly the way it happened." At another point, he had written, "I am running short of time, feel sick and tired, but . . . before I go beyond this world, I had to tell the truth." He had written it, he said "exactly the way it happened" because he felt he had played a crucial role in history—"We put LB Johnson as senator for Texas, and this position opened the road to reach the Presidency"—and he wanted it to be acknowledged. And there were other lines that leapt out. After he shot the man in Durango, he fled, and for years, he wrote, "I was to become the wandering Jew," until he met George Parr, who gave him the badge of a deputy sheriff and money and prestige, and "My life changed with the power invested in me." But most of all what leapt out were the details of the election night; as I read I realized that he was confirming the truth of everything other officials had said on the stand—things that he had, in 1948, denied, and that, because of his denial, had remained shrouded in uncertainty for the almost four decades since; that his manuscript answered all the questions that had been unanswered: why, for example, during that vote-altering done six days after the election, in addition to the two hundred extra votes for Johnson, Stevenson had been given two extra votes: he himself had not wanted to write down the names of the two hundred additional voters, Salas explained in the manuscript; "I did not want them in my handwriting," and instead had had one of his deputy election judges, Ignacio (Nachito) Escobar, do it, and "Nachito was a jolly man, full of jokes, he said, let us give this poor man [Stevenson] a *pilón* [gift]." As I leafed through the manuscript, I realized that Salas' confession—for that was what it was: a confession—solved all the mysteries that for so long had surrounded the election. "The people have a good reason not to believe what I wrote," he said in his manuscript. "The reason is that I lied under oath." Thanks to that manuscript, it would not be necessary for me, Robert Caro, to write, "No one will ever be sure if Lyndon Johnson stole it." He stole it.

*

I HARDLY DARED ask the question I had to ask. What if he said No? What proof would I have that at last, after so many years, there was confirmation of what had been, for all those years, denied? I knew that the Johnson people, who for almost forty years had attacked every attempt to prove that Lyndon Johnson stole the election, who had told so many lies about it, were going to lie and deny about this one. But I asked it: With my heart in my throat, I asked Mr. Salas if I could make a copy of the manuscript. He said I could, reiterating that he wanted history to know the truth. "Everyone is dead except me, Robert. And I'm not going to live long. But Box 13 is history. No one can erase that." He said there was a copying machine in a store not far away. We walked over and stood by the machine as, one by one, the pages slid out.

"Hell, no, he's not dead":
Vernon Whiteside

The articles and biographies about Lyndon Johnson had portrayed him as a popular, even charismatic, campus figure during his college years. When I started hearing these stories about how Lyndon Johnson stole an election for the Student Council, how he in effect blackmailed a girl opposing his candidate for the Council to get her to drop out of the election, how he was so unpopular on campus that his nickname was "Bull" (for "Bullshit") Johnson, I didn't believe them.

But I kept hearing them. I decided to interview more of his classmates.

Locating them proved to be quite a job. It had been only recently that the college—Southwest Texas State Teachers College in San Marcos—had begun keeping track of its former students, and it had no addresses for many of them, who seemed to be scattered all across America. And of course many of the women students had gotten married, and their names had changed, or had married and then divorced, and married again, so their names had changed more than once. Ina and I had to track them down, from one town or city to another.

Today, with a National Telephone Directory on your computer, it's easy to find people. But that didn't exist then. The New York Public Library had a little room with telephone directories not only for cities but for towns, too; sometimes the phone book for a place like, say, Johnson City, was a very slim volume. I remember sitting with Ina on the floor in this little room, with telephone books open on the floor all around us.

Eventually we found, and I interviewed, enough of these students so that I knew the stories—unsavory as they were—might well be true. But again and again, a student who was telling them to me would say he or she didn't know all the details. They would say that there was one student who did, who had worked closely with—had schemed with—Lyndon Johnson in college. His name was Vernon Whiteside. But everyone I talked to believed that Whiteside had died. Over and over I was told, "Well, old Whiteside, he would know about that. But old Whiteside is dead." (Actually, what I was hearing was, "Ol' Waatside, he daid.")

Then one day I telephoned a classmate of Lyndon's named Horace Richards. He lived in a small town near Corpus Christi, and I was calling to ask if I could drive down to see him. When he agreed, I told him some of the Johnson maneuvers I wanted to ask him about. He said he knew about them—in fact, had participated in some of them—but that he would tell me about them only if Vernon Whiteside also agreed to do so. I said: "But ol' Waatside, he daid."

"Hell, no," Richards replied. "He's not dead. He was here visiting me just last week."

Whiteside, Richards told me, had sold his ranch a year or two before, bought a fancy mobile home and had been driving around with his wife to see the United States, including Alaska, ever since; in that pre–cell phone time, he had been out of touch; that, I supposed, was why his classmates had thought him "daid." But, Richards said, ol' Vernon was planning to settle down now. When he had left Corpus Christi, he had been planning to drive to Florida and buy a condominium. Richards didn't know which city in Florida he was heading for. All he knew, he said, was that the city was north of Miami, and had "Beach" in its name.

That certainly narrowed it down some.

Oh, well. Ina and I got a map of Florida, and for each city or town north of Miami that had "Beach" in its name, we got the names of all its mobile home courts. We divided up the names, and started calling each court to see if a Whiteside was staying there. It was a court in Highland Beach, Florida, that said yes, there was, and indeed Mr. Whiteside had pulled in that very day, only a few hours before.

I didn't ask the court's operator to bring him to the phone. It's too easy to say no over the phone, and I wasn't going to give him the chance to say he didn't want to talk to me; the only flight to anywhere in Florida from Austin that evening was to an inconvenient city—I think it was Tampa—but I jumped in my car, drove to the airport, caught the flight, rented a car, and the next morning was knocking on his door. I told him my name and what I was doing, and said I'd like to talk to him, and he said, sure, come in—and over the course of many hours, with his wife sitting there listening, told me the details of the character-revealing episodes at which his classmates had hinted. And he told me of other episodes, of which only he knew. And when I made new calls to these men and women, they confirmed Whiteside's accounts, which added up to a portrait of the young Lyndon Johnson very different from the one previous accounts had depicted.

"It's all there in black and white":
Ella So Relle

A few days after I interviewed Mr. Whiteside, I spoke by telephone to another of Johnson's classmates, a woman who had retained her maiden name, Ella So Relle.

Ms. So Relle had become a schoolteacher, and her tone when she answered my questions (confirming those of the Whiteside incidents with which she was familiar) was the tart, acerbic tone she might have employed with a slightly backward pupil.

Finally, exasperated, she said, "I don't know why you're asking all these questions. It's all there in black and white."

"All *where* in black and white?" I asked.

In the *Pedagog*, she replied. I had read the *Pedagog*, the Southwest Texas yearbook, had found a copy for the year 1930, the year Lyndon Johnson had graduated, a large-size book thick with the ads of San Marcos merchants, had perused it, I had thought, thoroughly, and had found only a few references to Johnson, all innocuous, and certainly none which related to the Whiteside incidents. I asked Ms. So Relle if she had a copy of the yearbook—I had already observed, in the homes of many of the other Southwest Texas graduates I had visited, that the yearbook was often in a prominent place on their bookshelves, so important had their years there been to them—and of course she said she did. By this time I felt she was on the verge of hanging up on me, but I asked her if she would please—I know this is taking so much of your time, Miz So Relle, but it would mean so much to me—would she mind very much getting it and telling me the pages that contained the references? With a very audible sigh of resignation she went and got the yearbook. It wasn't hard for her to find those pages—they were all in a section of the yearbook called "The Cat's Claw"—and she read off the page numbers.

There were five of them: 210, 226, 227, 235, and 236. I turned the pages of my copy of the *Pedagog* to get to them—and they weren't there! The pages before and after them were there, but not 210, 226, 227, 235, or 236. Looking closely, I could see now that they had been cut out, but so carefully, and so close to the spine, perhaps with a razor, that unless you were looking as closely as I was, you wouldn't notice. I asked Ms. So Relle to read me what they said, but of course there was no hope of that, and the call was over.

I was in what I guess you could call a fever of impatience to see those pages, but the fever didn't last long. There was a used book store in San Marcos, and I had already noticed that they stocked old Southwest Texas yearbooks, and when I drove down there from Austin the next day there were several copies of the 1930 edition. In the first few I looked at, the five pages had been excised, but then I found one that had them, and Ms. So Relle had not been exaggerating: there was confirmation, in black and white, in print and in drawings, of the incidents of which Whiteside and others had spoken. Two of the five pages depicted the college elections that had been stolen under Lyndon Johnson's direction; one cartoon showed him hiding behind one of his candidates for the Student Council, another showed him and a group of his allies in the college's White Stars club standing in front of a photograph of a pile of wood on which a photograph of a black woman had been superimposed in what could only be an allusion to "a nigger in a woodpile"—shorthand for something crooked. And there was a question on those pages that was evidence of the mistrust with which he was regarded by his fellow students: "What makes half of your face black and the other half white, Mr. Johnson?" And there were three other pages dealing with him. On one was a reference to what his fellow students evidently believed was his determination to marry money (a fake advertisement to persuade students to join a Lonely Hearts Club entices him with the line "Lyndon, some of our girls are rich"); on another was an allusion to his loudness and untruthfulness; on the third a sarcastic reference to his penchant for flattering or "sucking up to" the faculty ("Believe It Or Not—Bull Johnson has never taken a course in suction"). I was holding in my hands—in that unexpurgated copy of his college yearbook—proof of the opinion of his peers about the young Lyndon Johnson.

"I wanted to be a citizen":
Margaret and David Frost

No choice at all. Just part of me, like it or not. Since the centerpiece of my third volume, a book about Lyndon Johnson as Senate Majority Leader, was going to be his monumental achievement in ramming through that body, in 1957, a bill to make it easier for black Americans to vote, the first civil rights bill to be passed in eighty-two years, I wanted to briefly show in the opening pages of the book—to make the reader understand and *feel* right at the beginning—how hard it had been for a black person to register to vote, let alone to actually cast a ballot, in the South before 1957: what were the obstacles facing African-Americans wanting to exercise this basic right of citizenship, the obstacles that Lyndon Johnson was going to fight to remove. To do so, I turned to testimony given by black men and women who had been denied that right before the passage of the bill. There was plenty of it, including that given to the United States Commission on Civil Rights in 1957 during a series of hearings in Montgomery, Alabama.

There was no shortage of dramatic testimony in the transcript of those hearings, but I finally decided to focus on that of thirty-eight-year-old Margaret Frost of the town of Eufala, in Alabama's Barbour County. I think the element of Mrs. Frost's story that got to me and made me want to tell it was that she had tried to register—had had a hearing before the three members of the Barbour County Board of Registrars, in January of 1957—and had been humiliated by them, and yet had tried again. The questions Mrs. Frost had been asked at that January hearing had been difficult, but she felt she had answered them all correctly. The board's chairman, William "Beel" Stokes, had rejected her application to register, however, telling her she had missed one—and had refused to tell her which one it was, saying only, "You all go home and study a little more." And despite the humiliation, Mrs. Frost *had* tried again, rehearsing, over and over, answers to all the questions the board might ask—and eight months later had gone down to the courthouse again (the hearings were held after hours in the County Clerk's office) and had been subjected again to humiliation: this time, there were three applicants, and while she and one of the others answered every question correctly, the third didn't, and Stokes therefore rejected all three applications, with the same words, "You all go home and study a little more." That got me, and so did the reason she gave the Civil Rights Commission when she was asked why she had again put herself at the board's mercy. "I was scared I would do something wrong," she said. "I was nervous. Shaky. Scared that the white people would do something to me [but] I wanted to be a citizen. I figure all citizens, you know, should be able to vote." I wanted to show the efforts black people had made to be part of the American political system, and how the system had prevented them from doing that, and with this story, I felt I could.

I telephoned her—her voice was soft, with a calm, dignified quality to it—and got more detail: how her husband, David, had helped her rehearse for the second hearing, how she had had no difficulty recalling, for the Civil Rights Commission, Beel Stokes' exact words because they were still vivid in her mind.

I asked her my questions: what was the hearing like? what did you see? Not much of a response at first, but, I pressed: when you were sitting there, what did the room look like?

We weren't sitting, she said. She and the other two applicants had stood in front of the counter at which, during the day, people stood while they were conducting their business with the county clerk. So the registrars were sitting behind the counter?, I asked. They weren't sitting either, she said. They were just standing behind the counter.

I understood why: my sentence would say, "No one offered them a chair, and the registrars didn't bother to pull up chairs for themselves, because the hearing wasn't going to take very long." I kept asking. What color were the walls? ("white—they needed a painting"). What decorations were hanging on them? (just photographs of county officials). I had enough details so that I should be able to make the reader visualize the dingy and plainly furnished—meanly furnished—room, and the contempt the registrars had had for the applicants: they hadn't even bothered to sit down. I had, from the transcript of her testimony, the words Beel Stokes had used. But what was Stokes' expression—what were the expressions on the three registrars as Stokes spoke these words? "You could see in their eyes they were laughing at us," Margaret Frost said.

I had all I needed: a good story, and enough details to make the reader see the setting in which it took place. Why did I say to myself: is there any more to the story? I *had* the story. Plenty of details. I kept saying to myself: schmuck, this is what you always do. You don't *need* any more details. This is the story you wanted: an example of the difficulties and humiliations that black Americans experienced when they tried to vote. You got it—now just write it. I wanted the reader to feel the indignation I felt at the way this dignified, soft-spoken woman had been treated, and I had enough detail so that if I could write the story well enough, it would accomplish that end.

Of course I deserve neither admiration nor censure (or, for that matter, contempt)—for not stopping there. There is still so much about myself that I don't understand, but, by putting down on paper these short recollections, I have come to understand that this was simply another instance, among so many, in which there were available to me no alternatives. I simply knew that I *couldn't write the Barbour County episode* without trying to find out if there was any more to it.

And of course there was: nothing that even resembled a big revelation, but a single additional incident. And as David Frost related it to me over the phone when I called back the Frost number and this time asked to speak to *him*, I felt that if I could include that incident and write it well enough, it would add a dimension to readers' understanding of the depths of the plight of black men and women in the South in the middle of the twentieth century. It wasn't just that they couldn't vote; if, because of their attempts to vote, they were persecuted, there was no one—literally, no one—to whom they could turn for help.

When I asked David Frost if he himself had ever attempted to register he said he had, some years before—and had in fact succeeded. But, he said, that had not turned out to be a happy experience for him. Previously, he said, white people in Eufala had always been friendly to him, had called him "David" or "Boy." But after he registered, they called him "Nigger," a word, he said, "I just hated, hated." And when whites heard that he was planning to actually cast a ballot on Election Day, he said, a car had pulled up in front of his house, and the men in it had shot out the lights on his porch. He had thought of calling the police, but as the car drove away, he saw that it was a police car.

Frost also gave me my first education—I was to get a lot more as I worked on the book over the next few years—about other tactics used in the white South to keep black people from voting: about, for example, the denial of "crop loans" by small-town bankers. Crop loans were the advance that cash-poor farmers needed each year to buy the seeds for the crop they were intending to plant. A black farmer who had registered to vote would go to the bank as usual for the loan—only to be told that this year there wouldn't be one, so that, often, he lost his farm. Lost his farm! So that he would have to, as I wrote, load his wife and children into his run-down car "and drive away, sometimes with no place to go." I was learning all right. And the story about the police car made me understand more deeply than before the full dimensions of what black Americans faced in the South: a situation where, when someone threatened you, you couldn't ask the police to protect you. There wasn't, really, anyone you could ask.

OF COURSE THERE WAS more. If you ask the right questions, there always is.

That's the problem.

"My eyes were just out on stems":
Lady Bird Johnson

There was only one topic about which, during an interview, I didn't ask a single question—or even dare to look at the person I was interviewing, who was Lady Bird Johnson. The topic was Alice Glass.

I had been intending to deal in only a few lines with the many women with whom Lyndon Johnson had had sex. This was less because of some ethical or moral conception of my responsibilities as author than because, although these "affairs" were numerous, none of them seemed to have any significance for him personally or to have any connection with his political or governmental activities.

Then, however, while turning pages in a folder whose label, "Public Activities–Biographic Information–Naval Career," hinted very strongly that turning pages in this folder would be a total waste of time, and whose contents seemed to consist largely of mimeographed copies of a press release about Johnson's activities in the Pacific in 1942, there was, suddenly, an age-browned Western Union form: CHARLES BELIEVES YOU SHOULD FILE FOR SENATE, it said. POLLS SHOW YOU LEADING. NO ONE ELSE SHARES HIS OPINION ENTHUSIASTICALLY. IF POSSIBLE, TELEPHONE. LOVE, ALICE MARSH.

I knew what the telegram was about because of another one,

which I had found in the Roosevelt Papers at Hyde Park. An election for a United States senator from Texas was going to be held in 1942, and Johnson wanted to enter the Democratic Primary, whose winner would almost certainly be elected in that then solidly Democratic state, instead of running for re-election to Congress. President Roosevelt, who had given his backing to the state's former governor, James V. Allred, didn't want him to. Johnson, who ordinarily would not have even considered defying FDR's wishes, had at first agreed to support the governor, but in May, 1942, was having second thoughts, and among the Roosevelt Papers was a copy of a telegram from presidential secretary Marvin McIntyre warning him very firmly to put them out of his mind. I knew who "Charles" was, of course. Charles Marsh was an individual crucially important to Johnson's early career since he was not only publisher of the only district-wide daily newspaper in Johnson's congressional district, but was also an immensely wealthy man with strong paternal feelings toward the young congressman. Trying to free Johnson from financial worries, he had already taken a step in that direction by selling him a tract of land in Austin at a price far below its value. Alice Marsh must be Charles' wife. But why, I wondered as I read the telegram, would she be telegraphing Johnson in Australia with political advice—advice that, whether or not the telegram was the reason, he had followed? I called for the "Marsh, Charles" folder in the "Selected Names" collection, and in it, amid many communications from Marsh to Johnson, was one, in August, 1942, from Marsh's wife. HOPE WE CAN HAVE THAT BIRTHDAY PARTY, it said.

About that time two other things happened, for the first of which I might give myself a little credit, the other of which was due to nothing but pure luck. Among the boxes for which Alan Hathway's stricture had proven repeatedly golden were those in the 12 boxes grouped together under the title "Pre-Presidential Confidential File," which, the library's description said, contained "'material taken from other files because it dealt with potentially sensitive areas." Among the letters and memoranda in Box 10 of this file, which mostly contained material dating from 1942, was a large manila envelope. On it, someone had written "To Be Opened Only By LBJ or JBC." Next to it in the file was what had been inside: a leather traveling portfolio containing four photographs, of an elegant, attractive woman. I had no idea who she was; I had never seen another picture of that person—and when I asked the archivists, none of them had, either. I couldn't ask "JBC," since at the time John Bowden Connally, Johnson's assistant at the time, had not yet consented to talk to me. That was the first of the two things. The second, which came out of nowhere, occurred not long thereafter. The telephone on the archivist's desk in the Reading Room rang, and the archivist said the call was for me, and when I picked up the phone it was the reception desk downstairs in the lobby, and the docent on duty said there were two women there who wanted to talk to me, and would I come down. I did, and one of the women said they had read *The Power Broker*, and therefore "We know you're going to find out about Alice," and she said she was Alice's sister. "I was her best friend," the other put in. The sister said, "We don't want her portrayed as just another bimbo. She was much, much more than that. We want to tell you about her." And the friend, Alice Hopkins, said, "Lyndon's relationship with her wasn't like anything else in his life."

Over coffee in the Villa Capri café, they told me about Alice, who was not at the time of the photographs actually Alice Marsh but still Alice Glass. And her sister, Mary Louise Glass, took out her wallet and showed me her photograph, which of course was a picture of the woman in the leather traveling portfolio upstairs, and told me that if I wanted to find out more about her I should go to their hometown, Marlin, and there talk particularly to Posh Oltorf, the Brown & Root lobbyist, who had been her close platonic friend.

Over the next few weeks, Ina and I drove up to that sleepy little town in the middle of nowhere several times, and heard enough to know that Alice Glass was in truth not just another bimbo, that although, as I was to write, "Alice Glass was from a country town . . . she was never a country girl," that she had come to Austin as a secretary to a state legislator, that, as one legislator recalled, "Austin had never seen anything like her," a woman a shade under six feet tall with reddish blond hair that, if she loosened it fell to her waist, creamy-white skin and features so classic that the famed photographer Arnold Genthe was to call her "the most beautiful woman" he had ever seen; that on the same night Charles Marsh met her, he left his wife and children and took her east, and that, when, on a trip to England, she saw the majestic eighteenth-century manor house called "Longlea," he built her a replica of it on a thousand-acre estate in the Virginia Hunt Country, where she led the Hazelmere Hunt ("the only thing Texas about Alice was her riding," a friend told me; "she could *really* ride"), and created a glittering salon of journalists and politicians—to which, in 1937, the new congressman from Texas was invited with Lady Bird, and soon began coming weekend after weekend. At first, her sister and her friend said, both Johnsons came, but soon, they said, "he would leave her on weekends, weekend after weekend," and come to Longlea, where "sometimes Charles would be there, and sometimes Charles wouldn't be there," because Lyndon and Alice had become lovers, in an affair that lasted for years, right under the nose of a man vitally important to Lyndon's career.

And I also heard enough to ascertain for myself that Lyndon Johnson's long affair with Alice was in fact unlike any affair he had with any other woman. The advice that Alice gave him—always to wear custom-made shirts with French cuffs and cuff links to make his long, ungainly arms look elegant rather than awkward; always to be photographed from the left side, because that side of his face looked better than the right; to wear Countess Mara neckties—he followed slavishly for the rest of his life. But it was the advice she gave him about politics that made the affair interesting to me; on one occasion, during that first year, 1937, she came up with a solution to a problem that, George Brown's chief lobbyist Posh Oltorf, his most trusted lawyer Ed Clark, and others told me, was threatening to end his congressional career almost before it began. Herman Brown, the fierce ruler of Brown & Root, had financed much of Johnson's first campaign for Congress, and was prepared to finance the rest of his career; Herman would shortly, as we have seen, be arranging for money to be given to Johnson to distribute to other congressmen, to give him his first toehold on national political power. But late in 1937, Herman and Lyndon were, Oltorf and Clark told me, on a "collision course," because while Johnson had secured some installments of the financing for the dam that Brown & Root was building outside Austin, he was also, in order to create a federal low-income housing project in that city, arranging for the city to condemn rental houses owned by Herman which were making him a good profit. He was refusing to back down, and Herman had had enough of the young congressman. "He was going to turn on Lyndon," Posh told me, "and if Herman turned on you, he would never turn back." And then Alice invited Lyndon and Herman to Longlea, and said to Marsh, "Why don't you fix things up between them? Why don't you suggest that they compromise—give Herman the dam, and let Lyndon have the land?" And the advice did indeed fix things up between them. Moreover, Posh and Ed Clark and (later) John Connally all told me, Alice had a political mind that made her advice on politics worth listening to, so much so that there were moments when her advice was decisive in Lyndon Johnson's decisions—as it had been in 1942, when she sent the telegram to him in Australia. That made the affair, to my thinking, significant enough to be included in my book. And it was, to my thinking, significant also because, as I was to write, it "juts out of the landscape" of Lyndon Johnson's life "as one of the few episodes in it, and perhaps the only one, that ran counter to his personal ambition"; he was, in the words of one observer, "taking one hell of a chance" with the man in his district perhaps most important to his continuation in office. And it demonstrated as well his talent for secrecy; his fawning over Marsh didn't let up during the years he was sleeping with Marsh's mistress, and Marsh's support of him, both editorial and financial, and his fondness for him, never faltered.

Moreover, as I learned, Alice's feelings toward Lyndon provide insight into certain aspects of his career. She fell in love with him, her sister and her best friend (and Posh Oltorf and others) told me, because, deeply idealistic herself, she was entranced by his stories, told over the dinner table and around the swimming pool at Longlea, of how hard life in the Hill Country was, and how he was getting the dams built and the electricity brought to make that life easier; she considered Lyndon an idealist, too, an idealist who knew how to get things done; "she thought," Mary Louise told me, "he was a young man who was going to save the world." But that concept endured only until he invited her out to the West Coast in 1942, when she became disillusioned by what I called "the contrast between Johnson's activities and the fact that he was supposed to be in a combat zone"; Posh showed me (and gave me a copy of) a letter she had written him in later years jokingly suggesting they write a book together on the true Lyndon Johnson: "I can write a very illuminating chapter on his military career in Los Angeles, with photographs, letters from voice teachers, and photographers." The passion eventually faded from the relationship, although perhaps not completely; Alice married Charles Marsh, but divorced him, and married, and divorced, several times after that; "she never got over Lyndon," Alice Hopkins said. Even when he was a senator, and vice president, he would drive down to Longlea to see her. But, Posh told me, Vietnam was too much for her; she had told him, Posh said, that she had burned love letters Johnson had written her, because she was ashamed of her friendship with the man she regarded as responsible for the escalation of the war.

ONE EVENING, our phone rang, and it was Posh. "Bird knows you've been to Marlin," he said in a panic-stricken voice. "So she knows you know about Alice."

At that time I was interviewing Mrs. Johnson every few weeks in her office at the Johnson Library, and I was scheduled to see her there that Saturday. On Friday, one of her secretaries came to my desk in the Reading Room. "Mrs. Johnson would like to see you at the ranch on Saturday," she said. "Come for lunch."

WE SAT IN the dining room, she at the head of the table, I at her right hand. The stenographer's notebook in which I took notes was to the right of my plate, and after she began talking, I didn't look up from it.

Without a word of preamble, she started talking about Alice Glass. She had known her slightly when she, Lady Bird, was a student at the University of Texas and Alice had been working in the Capitol, she said. Even then, Lady Bird said, "she was quite an intellectual girl and, you felt, destined for more exciting things than being a legislator's secretary." Then, she said, when "we saw them again in Washington, she was even prettier, and just dressed so beautifully. She was very tall, and elegant—really beautiful, in a sort of Amazonian way." I kept taking notes, my eyes down on my notebook. I found it impossible to look at her. She talked about Longlea. "My eyes were just out on stems," she said. "They would have interesting people from the world of art and literature and politics. It was the closest I ever came to a salon in my life. . . . There was a dinner table with ever so much crystal and silver." And she talked some more about Alice, about the contrast between Alice and her, with nothing in her voice but admiration: "I remember Alice in a series of long and elegant dresses, and me in—well, much less elegant." She talked about how Alice had given Lyndon such good advice, about cuff links, for example. "Lyndon always followed that." Lyndon followed religiously any advice Alice gave him, she said. There was no looking up. She kept returning to Alice's height and beauty. Once, she recalled, when Charles Marsh was talking about the threat the rising Adolf Hitler was posing for the world, she, Lady Bird, had said, "Maybe Alice can help us fight him. She's so tall and blond she looks like a Valkyrie." The admiration in her voice never wavered. I'm sure that I was too old to blush; I just, I am sure, *felt* as if I was blushing. The next week, we met in her office, for another long, immensely helpful, interview on other topics, during which I was able to look at her again.

Tricks of the Trade

Interviews: silence is the weapon, silence and people's need to fill it—as long as the person isn't you, the interviewer. Two of fiction's greatest interviewers—Georges Simenon's Inspector Maigret and John le Carré's George Smiley—have little devices they use to keep themselves from talking, and let silence do its work. Maigret cleans his ever-present pipe, tapping it gently on his desk and then scraping it out until the witness breaks down and talks. Smiley takes off his eyeglasses and polishes them with the thick end of his necktie. As for myself, I have less class. When I'm waiting for the person I'm interviewing to break a silence by giving me a piece of information I want, I write "SU" (for Shut Up!) in my notebook. If anyone were ever to look through my notebooks, he would find a lot of "SUs" there.

A Sense of Place

The importance of a sense of place is commonly accepted in the world of fiction; I wish that were also true about biography and history, about nonfiction in general, in fact. The overall quality, the overall level, of writing is, I believe, just as important in the one as in the other.

By "a sense of place," I mean helping the reader to visualize the physical setting in which a book's action is occurring: to see it clearly enough, in sufficient detail, so that he feels as if he himself were present while the action is occurring. The action thereby becomes more vivid, more real, to him, and the point the author is trying to make about the action, the significance he wants the reader to grasp, is therefore deepened as well. Because biography should not be just a collection of facts. Its base, the base of all history, of course *is* the facts, it's always the facts, and you have to do your best to get them, and get them right. But once you have gotten as many of them as possible, it's also of real importance to enable the reader to see in his mind the places in which the book's facts are located. If a reader can visualize them for himself, then he may be able to understand things without the writer having to explain them; seeing something for yourself always makes you understand it better.

Another point. Since places evoke emotions in people, places inevitably evoked emotions in the biographer's subject, his protagonist. Therefore, if a biographer describes accurately enough the setting in which an action took place, and if he has accurately enough presented the protagonist's character, the reader will be helped to understand the emotions that the setting evoked in the protagonist, and will better understand the significance that the action held for him. If the place is important enough in the subject's life—if he was raised in it, for example, or presided over it, or maneuvered within it—if the place played a significant role in shaping his feelings, drives and motivations, his self-confidence and his insecurities, then, by making the place real to the reader, the author will have deepened the reader's understanding of the subject, will have made the reader not just understand but empathize with him, feel with him.

In the case of Lyndon Johnson, two settings played a crucial role for me in grasping him and understanding his role in history, in understanding how he came to power and how he wielded power—two settings. The place he came from—the Texas Hill Country—and the place he came to when he was still a very young man: Capitol Hill.

The first place was really hard for me to understand. I am a New Yorker. I had spent my whole life here, in the city's crowded streets, crowded halls, with theaters, concerts, lively conversation all the time; to some extent I comprehend that world. But when I started working on the Johnson book, there was a 9:30 plane to Austin every morning and some mornings I'd be in New York in that world, take the plane, at the Austin airport rent a car, and drive west into the Texas Hill Country. And on the days that I did that, I felt I was going in the same day from one end of the world to the other. The geologic name for the Hill Country is the Edwards Plateau. It's 24,000 square miles—that's enough square miles to put all of New England into it and still have some miles left over. It starts at the western edge of Austin and stretches westward from there for more than three hundred miles. It's three hundred miles of one range of hills after another. The first settlers who came there called it the Land of Endless Horizons because every time they came to the top of one rise of hills there would be more rises stretching ahead.

Looking back on my work on Johnson, I think I realized on my very first drive into the Hill Country—or *should* have realized—that I was entering a world I really didn't understand and wasn't prepared for. I still remember: you drove west out of Austin, and about forty-one miles out you come to the top of a tall hill. And as I came to the crest of that hill, suddenly there was something in front of me that made me pull over to the side of the road and get out of the car and stand there looking down. Because what I was seeing was something I had never seen before: emptiness—a vast emptiness. I later found out that it's a valley, the valley of the Pedernales River. It's about seventy-five miles long and fifteen miles across. When I stood there looking down on it that first time, for a few minutes I didn't see a single sign of human beings in that immense space. Then something happened, the cloud moved from in front of the sun or whatever, and suddenly in the middle of this emptiness the sun was glinting off a little huddle of houses. That was Johnson City. When Lyndon Johnson was growing up in that town, there were 323 people there; when I got there, there were not that many more. As I stood on that hill, I realized that I was looking at something, was about to drive down into something, unlike anything I had ever seen before, in its emptiness, its loneliness, its isolation.

At that time Ina and I were working in the Johnson Library in Austin. We both worked from nine to five, when the library closed, and at five o'clock, I would hurry out to my car, and drive

out each evening into the Hill Country to interview one of the
men or women who had grown up with Lyndon Johnson or gone
to college with Lyndon Johnson or been part of his first political machine. He died so young, in 1973, at the age of sixty-four,
and I was starting the book in 1976, and most of the people were
still there who knew him, were still living in Johnson City, so I
could talk to them. For a while I thought these interviews were
just supplementary. As I said earlier, there were chapters on his
youth in the seven biographies of Johnson that had already been
published, so I thought I had enough material; I just needed some
more color, and I'd get it through these interviews. But when I
started talking to the people, I came to realize I was wrong about
that. That was when we decided to move to the Hill Country—to
a house west of Austin—and, as I've said, as soon as we moved out
there everything changed. People started to talk to you in a very
different way, and I started to get a whole different understanding
of what life had been like there when Lyndon Johnson was young,
and what the young Lyndon Johnson was like.

When I look back through the notebooks in which I took my
notes from the interviews with these men and women, I find
over and over the word "poor" written. There was a level of poverty there that a city person could hardly imagine. Some of the
families who lived outside the little towns that dotted the Hill
Country—Dripping Springs, Blanco, Junction, Telegraph—still
lived in the log dwellings called "dog-runs," which were two separate rooms or cabins connected under a continuous roof, with
an open corridor that had been left between them for ventila-
tion. That was where the dogs slept. When Lyndon Johnson was
growing up, there was very little cash in Johnson City. Very little.
You could get a dime for a dozen eggs, but you had to sell them in
Marble Falls, and Marble Falls was twenty-three miles away from

Johnson City. One of Lyndon Johnson's boyhood friends, Ben Crider, relates how he rode horseback the twenty-three miles between Johnson City and Marble Falls keeping the horse at a walk and carrying those dozen eggs in a box he held in front of him so that they wouldn't break, just for a dime. "Lonely" is a word that I found over and over again in my notes. (Just as in my notes on the scattered couples of East Tremont. But this was an even harsher kind of loneliness, a kind of loneliness hard to imagine—that *I* couldn't imagine, having grown up in New York City.) Lyndon Johnson didn't even grow up in Johnson City, small and isolated as it was; he grew up on the Johnson Ranch, which was fourteen miles beyond Johnson City, farther out into the hills. One corner of that ranch came down next to what they called the Austin–Fredericksburg Road, which was really not a road but only a graded, rutted path between these two places. Lyndon's little brother, Sam Houston Johnson, would tell me how he and Lyndon used to sit on the fence at that corner for hours when they were little boys hoping that a rider or carriage would come by so they'd have a new person to talk to.

Because I knew that their mother, Rebekah, was deeply unhappy due to her loneliness, and that Lyndon was affected by his mother's unhappiness, I felt that if I was going to understand him, I had to try to get a feeling for what such loneliness was like. So what I decided to do to get a taste, a tiny taste but still a taste, of such loneliness, was to spend a whole day alone in the hills, then spend the night there and wake up the next day and spend another with no one there but me. I took a sleeping bag—by that time, although I hadn't yet published a single word of my Johnson books, the Johnson family was deeply hostile to me, so I couldn't do it on the Johnson Ranch but I did it on a neighboring ranch—I spent a day there, and then I spent a night in a sleeping bag and the next day I spent there as well, and, you know, you find out things that you could never realize unless you did something like that. How sounds in the night, small animals or rodents gnawing on tree branches or something, can be so frightening; how important small things become. It was the things I learned in those two days that helped me to understand at least a little and to write

> When Rebekah walked out the front door of that little house, there was nothing—a roadrunner streaking behind some rocks with something long and wet dangling from his beak, perhaps, or a rabbit disappearing around a bush so fast that all she really saw was the flash of a white tail—but otherwise nothing. There was no movement except for the ripple of the leaves in the scattered trees, no sound except for the constant whisper of the wind. . . . If Rebekah climbed, almost in desperation, the hill in back of the house, what she saw from its crest was more hills, an endless vista of hills, hills on which there was visible not a single house . . . hills on which nothing moved, empty hills with, above them, empty sky; a hawk circling silently overhead was an event. But most of all, there was nothing human, no one to talk to.

And what about the nights? Lyndon's father, being a state legislator, was often away in Austin. I could make a better attempt now to at least try to imagine the feelings of a woman left alone at night with her children in that empty country. "No matter in what direction Rebekah looked," I wrote, "not a light was visible. The gentle, dreamy, bookish woman would be alone, alone in the dark—sometimes, when clouds covered the moon, in pitch dark—alone in the dark when she went out on the porch to pump water, or out to the barn to feed the horses, alone with the rustlings in the trees and the sudden splashes in the river which could be a fish jumping, or a small animal drinking—or someone coming." In trying to analyze and explain aspects of the character of the complicated man that was Lyndon Baines Johnson, you find a part of the explanation in the character of the harsh, lonely land in which he was raised.

It took me a long time to understand this—but during that time, there were moments of what were for me revelations, of insights that suddenly helped me understand.

ONE OF THESE MOMENTS had to do with his father—and with the effect on Lyndon Johnson of a mistake his father made because *he* didn't understand the land.

You can't get very deep into Johnson's life without realizing that the central fact of his life was his relationship with his father. His brother, Sam Houston, once said to me, "The most important thing for Lyndon was not to be like Daddy."

His father, Sam Ealy Johnson, looked remarkably like Lyndon. They were both over six feet tall, both had very big ears, both had that big jutting jaw and piercing dark eyes. And they both had the habit—Sam when he was in the Texas Legislature, Lyndon when he was in the House and Senate in Washington—of putting one arm around the shoulders of someone they were trying to persuade while grabbing the person's lapel with the other hand and holding him firmly and leaning into his face as they talked. And they were both master legislators. Sam, the father, was a very idealistic legislator, a legislator with a romantic streak, a legislator who felt that the purpose of government was to help people "caught in the tentacles of circumstance."

Sam was described as "a man of great optimism," and to some extent that optimism was justified in Austin: popular and skillful in the legislature, he got an impressive number of laws passed. But he also had to make a living, and he had to make it in the Hill Country. And his "optimism," his romantic, idealistic streak, kept him from looking at hard facts. In the Hill Country, that really cost him—cost him, among other things, the love, or at least the respect and admiration, of his elder son.

Generations before, during the 1870s and '80s, the era of the "Cattle Kingdom," there had been a great, sprawling Johnson Ranch along the Pedernales River from which huge herds had been driven up the Chisholm Trail to Abilene, with the original Johnson brothers returning with their saddle bags bulging with gold. But the family had ceased making money and had lost the ranch some decades before Lyndon was born in 1908 and now, when Lyndon was about ten years old, it came on the market, and Sam Johnson determined to buy it—to re-create the original "Johnson Ranch," to make the whole Pedernales Valley "Johnson Country" again.

One reason that the ranch had been lost, however, was that its soil had worn out, had washed away when cattle grazed on it, or, later, when attempts were made to grow cotton on it, and there was no longer much soil left on top of the limestone base. You couldn't do anything with the land. It still looked beautiful and fertile—when you go out to the ranch today, the grass covers those rolling hills; there are still big, majestic live oak trees with their shiny leaves. But beautiful as it was when Sam looked at it, there wasn't going to be any way of making much money out of that land. And Sam didn't realize that. Seeing how beautiful it was, he had this romantic dream of restoring the great Johnson Ranch, and so he believed he was going to make it pay, and, to outbid other people, he overpaid for the ranch. He paid so much that the ranch couldn't possibly earn back what he paid for it. And very quickly, when Lyndon was fourteen, Sam went broke and lost the ranch. And a crucial element of Lyndon Johnson's youth is a consequence of that loss: the insecurity that followed. The family—Sam and Rebekah, the two boys and the girls, Rebekah, Josefa, and Lucia—moved to a little house in Johnson City. Every month, Lyndon had to live with the fear that the bank was going to take that house away. He lived in a house in which his father, broken by his financial failure, was constantly ill, and there was often no food, and neighbors brought covered plates. Worst of all, perhaps, his father became the laughingstock of the town, an object of ridicule ("Sam Johnson is a mighty smart man. But he's got no sense") in the speeches given at political barbecues as his son stood listening. When Lyndon Johnson was eighteen and nineteen years old, he worked for almost two years on a highway gang driving a Fresno. People in New York can't even imagine what a Fresno is. A Fresno is the device that was used to grade—to level—these unpaved highways back then. It's a big, heavy slab of iron with the front edge sharpened. Handles have been soldered on to each side. The driver of a Fresno puts a hand on each handle, and as a team of mules pulls, he pushes the sharp edge of the iron slab through the ground, a caliche soil hard to begin with and baked even harder by the sun. And because both his hands are occupied, one on each handle, he loops the reins and ties them behind his back so that, as I wrote, Lyndon Johnson was really in harness with the mules for hours every day. He lived with his father's mistake, his father's one great mistake, all his youth.

When I began *The Path to Power*, I had this romantic idea about Sam, that he was such a great legislator, fighting for people and all. Then one day Lyndon's cousin Ava, his favorite cousin, said to me—I could tell she really didn't like it when I talked about Sam in so admiring a way—she said, "Let's drive out to the Johnson Ranch." So we drove out to the Johnson Ranch and you got there and that grass-covered landscape looks beautiful, and fertile. And she said, "Now, get out of the car." I got out of the car. Ava was an old woman but a very forceful woman. She said, "Now kneel down," and I knelt down, and she said, "Now stick your fingers into the ground." And I stuck my fingers into the soil and I couldn't even get them into the ground the length of my finger. There was hardly any soil on top of that rock. There was enough to grow the beautiful grass but not enough to grow cotton or graze cattle. Ava said to me, "Do you understand now? Sam didn't really see. He didn't want to see. It looked so beautiful." In other words, she was saying, he didn't see the reality of it. The reality—the hard unblinking facts. He deluded himself.

Now what's the relationship of this to Lyndon Johnson's political activities? Of all his political abilities—and he had so many remarkable political abilities—one of the most remarkable was his ability to count votes. To know in advance which way a congressman or a senator—and during his six years as Majority Leader, he had to know *every* senator because he was often operating with a one-vote majority, 48 Democrats, 47 Republicans and Wayne Morse, an independent—to know how every senator was going to vote on a particular motion or piece of legislation. Vote-counting—accurate vote-counting: to be right in your count, when you *have* to be right—is a very rare ability. Sometimes a senator will mislead his Leader—the Majority or Minority Leader—about how he's going to vote, or will say he's undecided himself and isn't going to decide until the last minute, or even until the roll call itself has begun, and sometimes a senator is torn between conflicting pressures or beliefs. One day he feels he's going to vote Aye and the next day he feels he's going to vote Nay. Sometimes a senator doesn't know himself until the very last minute where he's going to come down.

And there's another reason vote-counting is difficult, which relates particularly to the place of Lyndon Johnson's youth. Vote-counting is not only a vital political art but one that's really hard to master. Very few people can master it because, as I put it in *Master of the Senate*, it is an art "peculiarly subject to the distortions of sentiment and romantic preconceptions. A person psychologically or intellectually convinced of the arguments on one side of a controversial issue feels that arguments so convincing to him must be equally convincing to others." And therefore, as one of Johnson's vote-counters put it, "Most people tend to be much more optimistic in their counts than the situation deserves. . . . True believers were always inclined to attribute more votes to their side than actually existed." But Lyndon Johnson never had that problem. His father had been the man of optimism—"great optimism." Lyndon had seen firsthand, when his father failed, the cost of optimism, of wishful thinking. Of hearing what one wants to hear. Of failing to look squarely at unpleasant facts. Because his father purchased the Johnson Ranch for a price higher than was justified by the hard financial facts, Lyndon Johnson had felt firsthand the consequences of romance and sentiment. Optimism—false optimism: for many people, it's just an unfortunate personal characteristic. For Lyndon Johnson, it was the bite of the reins into his back as he shoved, hour after hour, under that merciless Hill Country sun, pushing the Fresno through the sun-baked soil.

Of all the aspects of Lyndon Johnson that impressed people when he arrived in Washington, vote-counting came first. Over and over when I was interviewing in Washington someone would say to me, He's the greatest vote-counter who ever lived. James H. Rowe, Jr., was a Washington insider for thirty years, the trusted, powerful adviser to Democratic presidents starting with Franklin Roosevelt. And he met Johnson when Johnson came to Washington as a congressman in 1937. He told me that even in those early days, Johnson was the very best at counting. He would figure it out—how so-and-so would vote . . . What—what exactly—would swing him." He tried to teach his staffers, as Majority Leader he would send them to talk to senators, find out which way they were going to vote, and report back to him. And the report that got him—you can't say angriest, because he was often angry, he was often flying into ferocious rages—but the report that would invariably set off one of these rages was one from a staffer who came back and said something like "I think he's going to vote this way." Johnson would say, snarl at him really, "What good is *thinking* to me? I need to *know*!" Bobby Baker, who was his chief vote-counter, said, "He never wanted to be wrong, *never*. I learned I had better *never* be wrong."

This vote-counting ability would be described to me in terms of awe, because no one quite understood where it came from. People would tell me it was almost supernatural, the way he knew how every senator would vote. In fact that's the word that was sometimes used to me in Washington: Lyndon Johnson's vote-counting ability was almost "supernatural." Yet because of my trip to the Johnson Ranch with Ava, I felt that Lyndon Johnson's genius for vote-counting was in some ways the very opposite of supernatural—that to some extent "natural" would be the best word to describe it. Rooted in nature. A product of the place, created in the place, that Lyndon Johnson was from: that Texas Hill Country. It was the Hill Country that taught him how terrible could be the consequences of a single mistake. When he was counting votes in the Senate he used to stand in the center of the Senate cloakroom holding one of those Senate tally sheets. Aides and senators would be coming up to him and he'd be counting the votes, his thumb moving down the list of senators and pausing at the name of each senator. And, I was told, his thumb would never move until he *knew* how that senator would vote. If you want to understand what was behind him doing that, think of the land. Think of the *place*. Think of the sheer ruthlessness, the unforgivingness, of the place. The Hill Country wasn't a city where at least you have welfare and some other social services to cushion your fall if you fail. You failed in the Hill Country, on your farm or ranch, you lost the place where your family lived, you might have to pack your wife and children into your car and drive off, "sometimes," as I wrote, "with no place to go."

A senator from the state of Washington, Henry (Scoop) Jackson, served with Johnson as senator and under the presidencies of both John Kennedy and Johnson. He was asked once, "What was the difference between Kennedy and Johnson?" and Jackson said, "Well, you know Kennedy was so charming. If he needed a senator's vote he would have him down to the White House. He would explain how badly he needed the vote. But if the senator said that if he gave him this vote, it would ruin him in his state, it would ruin him with his constituency, Kennedy would understand.

"Lyndon Johnson," Scoop Jackson said, "wouldn't understand. He would refuse to understand. He would threaten you, would cajole you, bribe you or charm you, he would do whatever he had to. But he would get the vote." I felt I understood that. Because being charming, being friends, wasn't what mattered to Johnson. What mattered to him was winning, because he knew what losing could be, what its consequences could be.

Hundreds of writers—journalists and the authors of books—all agree that Lyndon Johnson was ruthless. I try to explain *why* he was ruthless—and a large part of the explanation is the place he came from.

AND HOW ABOUT the place he came *to:* Capitol Hill? He first came there in December, 1931, as a twenty-three-year-old assistant to a Texas congressman. In his whole life, he'd had only one ambition but it was going to have to start on Capitol Hill. When he was on that road gang driving the Fresno and the road gang broke for lunch and was sitting around eating, he would start telling the other men about how he was going to be President of the United States one day. Jim Rowe once said to me, "From the moment he got here, there was only one thing he wanted: to be President." But when I began talking to the people who knew Lyndon Johnson when he started out in Washington as a congressional assistant, it seemed to me as if I was again missing something, like I had missed something at first in the Hill Country: something vague, but important; that there was something crucial that I wasn't adequately describing in my writing. I wasn't fully understanding what these people were telling me about the depth of Lyndon Johnson's determination, about the frantic urgency, the desperation, to get ahead, and to get ahead fast. As if the passions, the ambitions that he brought to Washington, strong though they were, were somehow intensified by the fact that he was finally *there*, in the place where he had always wanted to be. I wanted, I guess, to show in terms of Washington, to show in terms of Capitol Hill, the contrast between what he was coming from—the poverty, the insecurity, the land of dog-run log cabins—and what he was trying for.

I first got a clue about how I might be able to do this by talking to the young woman who worked with him as the other assistant in that congressman's office, a woman named Estelle Harbin. I asked her what he had been like and she described him. It was a vivid description. She called him a real tall thin boy, he was gangling, he was skinny, he was awkward, those big ears sticking out, his clothes didn't fit him well, he had long arms and the sleeves were never long enough, and his wrists were always sticking out of the cuffs. (Alice Marsh, the sophisticated mistress who taught him to wear cuff links was still some years in the future.) He was very poor, Ms. Harbin told me. He arrived in Washington in December, 1931, with a cardboard suitcase and only one coat, a thin topcoat not adequate for Washington winters. I asked Ms. Harbin what would he say to you and she said, Well, he couldn't stop talking about his train ride to Washington. He would say, "Have you ever ridden in the Pullman [a sleeping car]? I never did until I went up." "Have you ever eaten in a dining car? I never did." When he received his first monthly paycheck he told Miss Harbin that he wanted to deposit it in a bank but that he didn't know how to open a bank account: He had never had one. She also told me how quickly Lyndon Johnson learned, how desperate he was to learn, how he became, so quickly, in her words "the best congressional assistant there ever was."

One thing that got me was her saying that when he came to work in the morning he was always out of breath because he had been running. He lived in this little hotel, the Dodge Hotel, down Capitol Hill by Union Station. His office was in the House Office Building on the opposite side of Capitol Hill, so his route to work would be to come up from that hotel, up Capitol Hill, and then to come along in front of the entire long east façade of the Capitol, before continuing down on the other side to the

House Building. Estelle Harbin lived somewhere behind the Library of Congress, and sometimes she would be coming to work and she would see Lyndon Johnson coming up Capitol Hill. And she said to me that every time he got in front of the Capitol he would start running. Well, I wanted the reader to feel all this. I wanted not just to say that he was coming from poverty, the land of little dog-run cabins, and was trying for something monumental. I wanted to make the reader *see* the contrast between what he was coming from and what he was trying for—to see the majesty and the power of what he was trying for. I wanted to make the reader see this and *feel* this as Lyndon Johnson saw and felt it. I kept thinking that the key to doing that, to showing that, was somehow on that walk along Capitol Hill. So I kept taking that walk over and over again—I don't know how many times I took it, but it was a lot of times—but I didn't see anything there. Yet obviously something on that walk had excited him and thrilled him so much that he'd break into a run every morning. And I wasn't seeing anything that would account for that.

Then something occurred to me. Although I had taken this walk a lot of times, I had never done it at the same hour that Lyndon Johnson took it, which was very early in the morning, about 5:30 in the summers, about 6:30 in winter. Since he and Estelle had been raised on ranches, they got up with the sun. I decided to try doing that to see if there was something, and there was. It was something I had never seen before because at 5:30 in the morning, the sun is just coming up over the horizon in the east. Its level rays are striking that eastern façade of the Capitol full force. It's lit up like a movie set. That whole long façade—750 feet long—is white, of course, white marble, and that white marble just *blazes* out at you as that sun hits it. And then I felt I had found a way not to lecture the reader on the contrast between what Lyndon

Johnson was coming from and what he was striving toward, and how that contrast helped explain the desperation, the frenzied, frantic urgency of his efforts—a way not to tell the reader but to *show* the reader that point instead. I don't know whether I succeeded in doing that or not, but for what it's worth here's what I wrote about when Lyndon Johnson first came to Washington.

He lived in the basement of a shabby little hotel, in a tiny cubicle across whose ceiling ran bare steam pipes, and whose slit of a window stared out, across a narrow alley, at the weather-stained red brick wall of another hotel. Leaving his room early in the morning, he would turn left down the alley onto a street that ran between the red brick walls of other shabby hotels. But when he turned the corner at the end of that street, suddenly before him, at the top of a long, gentle hill, would be not brick but marble, a great shadowy mass of marble—marble columns and marble arches and marble parapets, and a long marble balustrade high against the sky. Veering along a path to the left, he would come up Capitol Hill and around the corner of the Capitol, and the marble of the eastern façade, already caught by the early-morning sun, would be a gleaming, brilliant, almost dazzling white. A new line of columns—towering columns, marble for magnificence and Corinthian for grace—stretched ahead of him, a line . . . of columns, so long that columns seemed to be marching endlessly before him . . . the long friezes above them crammed with heroic figures. And columns loomed not only before him but above him—there were columns atop columns, columns in the sky. For the huge dome that rose above the Capitol was circled by columns not only in its first mighty upward thrust, where it was rimmed by thirty-six great pillars (for the thirty-six states that the Union had comprised when it was built), but also high above, three hundred feet above the ground, where, just below the statue of Freedom, a circle of thirteen smaller, more slender shafts (for the thirteen original states) . . . add[ed] a grace note to a structure as majestic and imposing as the power of the sovereign state that it had been designed to symbolize. And as Lyndon Johnson came up Capitol Hill in the morning, he would be running.

Sometimes, the woman who worked with him, coming to work in the morning, would see the gangling figure running awkwardly, arms flapping, past the long row of columns on his way to the House Office Building beyond the Capitol. At first, because it was winter and she knew that he owned only a thin topcoat and that his only suits were lightweight tropicals suitable for Houston, she thought he was running because he was cold. . . . But in Spring, the weather turned warm. And still, whenever she saw Lyndon Johnson coming up Capitol Hill, he would be running.

Well, of course he was running—from the land of dog-run cabins to this. Everything he had ever wanted, everything he had ever hoped for, was there. And that gigantic stage lit up by the brilliant sun, that façade of the Capitol—that *place*—showed him that. Showed him that, and if I could write it right, would show the reader as well.

Two Songs

ow I'm working on the final volume of the Johnson biography. I was thinking about Winston Churchill recently, because Churchill wrote a biography of his great ancestor, Lord Marlborough, and someone once asked Churchill how it was coming along, and he said, "I'm working on the fourth of a projected three volumes." I'm not comparing myself to Winston Churchill, of course, but in this one way we're sort of in the same boat. I'm working on the fifth of a projected three volumes.

The fifth book, in a way, is a coming together of everything I've been trying to do, because never has there been a clearer example of the enormous impact—both for good and for ill—that political power has on people's lives than during the presidency of Lyndon Johnson. On one side, the Civil Rights Act, the Voting Rights Act, Medicare, Medicaid, Head Start, a liberal immigration bill, some seventy different education bills—they're all passed during the 1960s by President Lyndon Johnson. At the same time, Vietnam: that's a story that comes to swallow up so much else. Vietnam is 58,000 American dead, and more than 288,000 seriously wounded Americans. Thousands have to live without a leg or an arm for the rest of their lives. And we weren't even focused on post-traumatic stress disorder back then. Thousands—probably tens of thousands—of other men lived all their lives with PTSD. Vietnam—that's political power too.

I do most of the research for a book before I start writing, but this volume has been different because on Vietnam the LBJ Library is opening up new files all the time. People are always asking me what my daily schedule is. It's not fixed. I write each day as long as I can. As I've said, I write my first drafts in longhand—pen or pencil—on white legal pads, narrow-lined. I seldom have only one draft in longhand—I'd say I probably have three or four. Then I do the same pages over on a typewriter. I used to type on what they called "second sheets," brownish sheets, cheap paper like the paper used in the *Newsday* city room when I was a reporter. But those sheets are letter size. When I started writing books, I switched to white legal-size typing paper. You can get more words on a page that way. I triple-space the lines the way I did as a newspaperman, so there will be plenty of room to rewrite in pencil. I rewrite a lot. Sometimes I look at a page I typed but have reworked in pencil, and there's hardly a word in type left on it. Or no words in type left at all—every one has been crossed out. And often there's been so much writing and rewriting and erasing that the page has to be tossed out completely. At the end of the day there will be a great many crumpled-up sheets of paper in the wastepaper basket or on the floor around it.

I used to work late in the day or even into the evening, but as I've gotten older I've had to accept the fact that I'm just not able to work the same way. I always start each day by reading what I wrote the previous day, and more and more frequently when I reread the stuff I wrote in the late afternoon the day before, it was no good and I had to throw it out. So there was no sense in working late; I stop earlier now.

I get too wound up when I'm working. Concentrating too hard or something. Any interruption is a shock, a real jolt. In what I regard as a shameful episode in my writing career, I was typing away in the Frederick Lewis Allen Room at the Public Library when I got tapped on the shoulder by someone wanting me to go to lunch with him. I found myself on my feet with my fist drawn back to punch the guy—an elderly mild-mannered gentleman who was cringing in front of me—before, in the nick of time, I got a grip and apologized. I used to unwind at the end of a day by pouring myself several inches of a single-malt Scotch or a Kentucky sour mash called "Weller 107" (for 107 proof) as soon as I got home, and sipping it as I went through the mail. But some years ago I had an illness and can't drink anymore. The doctor asked me if I would miss it, and I said no; I lied. Sometimes when I come home, Ina takes one look at my face and says, "Boy, I wish you could still drink."

(Some of my friends may feel differently. Weller 107 was a very special sour mash. So few bottles were manufactured each year—each bottle was numbered by hand—that there would be only a few for sale in any one liquor store, or, indeed, in any one city. It was the favorite beverage of a powerful southern senator, Richard Brevard Russell of Georgia, whose support was vital to the career of Lyndon Johnson and the balance sheet of Brown & Root. As soon as Russell had accepted Johnson's annual invitation to visit the Johnson Ranch, Lyndon would call George Brown of Brown & Root, and Brown would dispatch the Brown & Root lobbyist, Posh Oltorf, in the company plane from city to city until three cases—thirty-six bottles—of 107 were assembled for Lyndon to give Russell as a gift to take back to Georgia with him. Once, when I won a literary prize, Posh, who had become my good friend, sent me three cases of Weller 107. When the doctor gave me the verdict on my drinking, I distributed the remaining bottles to friends. I kept two bottles from which I offer drinks to my very closest friends; it is almost all gone now.)

THEY SEEM TO BE publishing books on Vietnam faster than I can read them, but you can also learn from the telephone tapes and Johnson's papers and from interviewing the people who were there, inside the White House, how it happened, how we got into Vietnam and kept getting in deeper and deeper. And in domestic affairs—like civil rights—his political genius is just fascinating. On the telephone tapes you can hear this genius in action.

THIS VOLUME IS about Lyndon Johnson in the Sixties, so of course it's not only about Johnson but about the Sixties themselves. America at the end of the 1960s was a very different country from what it was at the beginning of that decade. Sometimes I find myself thinking of the Sixties in terms of the decade's protest songs—the great protest songs. I recall a friend, Louise Mirrer, saying, "What I remember about the Sixties is standing outside of Carnegie Hall with my mittens on, freezing, trying to get tickets to the protest concerts there." Well, I was also standing on those lines, trying to hear the Weavers and Pete Seeger. I don't believe (and I certainly hope) that I wasn't wearing mittens, but when Louise said that, I realized that to me also, in a way, songs define and sum up that decade—particularly two songs.

One is a song that had been sung for a long time before the 1960s. It's "We Shall Overcome," of course. We all know it, maybe some of you actually sang it when you were young, holding hands with the people alongside you. I wrote a few pages about it in Book Two of my Johnson biography, *Means of Ascent*, saying that that song had been sung for a very long time before the Sixties, that it was a hymn that was sung at the beginning of the nineteenth century, probably even earlier, in African-American churches. Sung probably by people who were slaves. The thing about this song is that even then, as I wrote, it was a song of defiance, of defiance and demand. In those earliest written descriptions of it is the line "We shall not yield." And when, in the 1940s, it began to be sung not only in churches but on picket lines, it was still a song of defiance and demand. During one strike, by black women workers against a company that simply seemed too strong for them to possibly have a chance to win, the strike went on for a long time, and they weren't winning. To keep their courage up, they started singing that church hymn, and added two lines: "We will win our rights," and "We will overcome." They kept picketing—and eventually won.

Then, during the 1950s, it was taught at the Highlander Folk School in Tennessee, a school created to teach people how to organize in the labor unions, and to teach civil rights workers how to fight for their cause. The legendary folksinger Pete Seeger came to sing it there. Two things happened. He changed "We will overcome" to "We shall overcome." That change shows the power of words. Changing a single word—changing "We will overcome" to "We shall overcome"—makes a big difference to the song. I also wrote in *Means of Ascent* about another thing that Seeger said: that as he was singing it, and black audiences were singing along with him, "I felt as if I were singing it too fast, as if they were tugging at the rhythm." And, he said, "I thought I'd better stop playing my banjo and just let them sing." And as they sang, I wrote, "they slowed it back down to its original stately, solemn, powerful meter, appropriate to its mighty words." "We shall overcome, / we shall overcome, some day. / Oh, deep in my heart, / I do believe / We shall overcome, some day."

"We Shall Overcome" began to be sung a lot more at the beginning of the Sixties because in a way "We Shall Overcome" *is* the 1960s. 1960 was, as I wrote, "the year of the first sit-ins to desegregate department store lunch counters in Southern cities. The young, neatly dressed blacks, sworn to nonviolence, sitting on the counter stools were taunted in attempts to make them relinquish their seats. . . . Police arrived, arrested them and flung them into paddy wagons. But they got their breath back, and as the wagons drove off, from their barred windows could be heard: 'Deep in my heart / I do believe / We shall overcome some day.' "

So during the next years, as I wrote, the hymn was sung in a thousand sit-ins, during a hundred Freedom Rides. A new verse, "We'll walk hand in hand," was added. Civil rights workers would cross their arms and with each hand, clasp the hand of the persons standing next to them, and sway rhythmically as they sang. Black hands were more and more clasping white, and there was another verse: "Black and white together." In August, 1963 at the March on Washington, which its organizers had been afraid would be poorly attended, a quarter of a million people sang it in the nation's capital. That, I think, was the moment when "We Shall Overcome" became the anthem of the civil rights crusade of the 1960s.

As I'm writing these books, I'm always watching newsreels to try and get a feel for what happened at certain moments. And there are some unbearable moments in the newsreels of the 1960s, unbearable to me anyway, and so many of them include, I realized, "We Shall Overcome." One you may remember is when a black church was bombed in Birmingham, and four little black girls were killed. The newsreel cameras weren't allowed inside the church; they're outside. Watching the film, you see the crowd outside the church, and one of the things you see is that this is quite a large crowd. It's not only the people from the community who couldn't fit into the church, but there are an awful lot of people from other cities and towns who came to this funeral. Not just black people. And what you see, what you hear, what you feel, is the absolute silence of this crowd. And then the pallbearers start to bring out the four little coffins. They bring them out into that silence. And then a woman—one woman begins to sing "We Shall Overcome." And other people join in. And, as I wrote, "over the sobs of mothers rose up the words: 'We shall overcome some day.'" I wrote a few pages about "We Shall Overcome" in Book Two. I'm going to write a lot more about it in Book Five. The writing will have to be pretty good to capture what that song meant, but I'm going to try.

I'VE BEEN ENCOUNTERING questions of race, of segregation—of America's great crime—all my professional life. When I was a young reporter, working nights for *Newsday* on Long Island, my beat was a series of towns, and what you did, among other things, was you checked the police stations in each of these towns every night. And during my first week on the job, I read a police report of an incident that had occurred that day on Northern Boulevard on Long Island, which is a busy thoroughfare. A man had run out into the street—he had been caught in bed with another man's wife and the husband chased him out, naked, ran after him and shot him dead in the middle of Northern Boulevard. I thought I had a good story, an up-front story. I went back and told the editor. He liked the story. But then he said, "Wait a minute, is that black on black?" Meaning was it a crime that involved only African-Americans? I said it was. And he said, "Give me three or four paragraphs. We'll put it inside."

THE HEROISM OF THE PEOPLE who fought for civil rights in the streets during the Sixties is monumental, but in talking about the Civil Rights Act of 1964, that heroism shouldn't be all that we talk about. Because there had been moments before, many moments before, in fact, when national indignation had boiled up over civil rights, and during many of those moments, there had also been liberal majorities in Congress. And dozens—scores—of civil rights bills had been introduced, but none had been passed until Johnson passed the weak one of 1957, and an even weaker one in 1960. Something more was needed.

The something more was Lyndon Johnson. When you talk about Lyndon Johnson, you're talking about a very complicated guy. He came to Congress in 1937. Between 1937 and 1957, his record was one of opposition, 100 percent opposition; he voted against every civil rights bill that was ever introduced, including anti-lynching bills. But it wasn't just that he voted with the South. He was a southern strategist, working with Richard Russell of Georgia. "A Russell of the Russells of Georgia," is what I titled my chapter on him because he was so proud of his heritage, proud of "the Old South," a racist in the deepest, cruelest sense of the word, a man seething with hatred toward blacks. He was the leader of the really all-powerful "Southern Caucus," the Southern Bloc in Congress that for literally decades had kept any meaningful civil rights legislation from passing. Lyndon Johnson convinced Russell that he believed the same way Russell did. Russell made him his protégé and began to elevate him to power in the Senate.

I remember talking to Ralph Yarborough, who was Johnson's Texas colleague in the Senate, asking him why the southerners were supporting Johnson. And he said, "He made them think that he was with them and that he'd be with them forever." I remember how I found out for myself how deeply he had made them believe this. I was trying to interview all the southern senators who were alive and their aides, and I'd been trying for years to interview Herman Talmadge of Georgia, who had served three terms in the Senate. He was another of the people who had never responded to my letters, and when I would call his office, he'd never call me back. Finally, in the year 2000, out of nowhere, he suddenly got in touch with me and said he would see me. I had heard he was very ill—dying, in fact—and, as I found out, indeed he was. But he said to come down and see him.

On the trip there, you got a picture of the power of the Talmadges in Georgia, where Herman Talmadge's father, Eugene Talmadge, had three terms as governor (he was elected to a fourth, but died before he was inaugurated). Gene Talmadge was known as "Whipping Gene" (while he hadn't ever joined the Ku Klux Klan, he said, "I used to do a little whipping myself"). Senator Talmadge said I should fly to Atlanta and he'd send someone to the Atlanta airport to pick me up. I thought he'd send some kid to drive me down. Instead he sent a top official of the state Democratic Party. This guy himself gave me a taste of the South on the way down because first of all he didn't like being sent on that errand; in the second place, my name is Caro, so he thought I was Catholic and that was bad enough, but on the way down I made sure to say I was Jewish. So it was a long drive.

Anyway, to get to see Herman Talmadge, you drive south out of Atlanta on Herman Talmadge Highway. You get off at the exit marked "Herman Talmadge Boulevard." You drive on Herman Talmadge Boulevard to Lake Talmadge. And there's this big house with tall white columns and when you ring the doorbell a black man in a waistcoat comes to the door and says, "The Senator is waiting for you in the library." I thought, "This is a scene from *All the King's Men*, and I'm Jack Burden."

The senator was indeed very ill and in my notes on the conversation I wrote down many times "a long pause," "long pause." Talmadge said about Lyndon Johnson, "At first, for years, I liked him. He spent a long time cultivating me, hours and hours. We would talk about everything: hunting, girls, civil rights." I asked him how did Johnson view the relationship between whites and Negroes. He said, "Master and servant." So I asked, Well didn't Johnson have any sympathy for blacks, any desire to improve their lot? My notes say "long pause." And then I wrote his two-word reply: "None indicated." Another pause, and then: "He was with us in his heart. I believed him. I believed him."

NO ONE MEANINGFUL CIVIL RIGHTS BILL—no bill with effective enforcement teeth in it—had been passed since 1875. Not since Reconstruction. So in 1964, when Lyndon Johnson became President, no strong civil rights bill, no meaningful civil rights bill had been passed in eighty-nine years.

John F. Kennedy had introduced a bill, a strong bill, in June of 1963. His speech introducing it was very moving, but when he was assassinated on November 22, five months later, the bill wasn't moving—and it wasn't going to move. Congress had stopped it cold.

And looking at Lyndon Johnson's passage of that Civil Rights Act of 1964, watching how he got it through Congress, trying to understand how he did it, how he did something that no one had been able to do, at least not for all those decades, taught me some things, things about which I had had no idea, about a particular form of political power: legislative power. And about legislative genius, too—genius in its highest sense, with the greatest significance, because what he accomplished wasn't merely the passage of an Act, a bill, a piece of legislation. It was a step—a big step—toward justice. That's why I tried first to figure out, then to explain, how Lyndon Johnson managed to do it. Hard to figure it out, hard to explain it. Harder to do it.

THE LIFE OF LYNDON JOHNSON is in many ways, to me anyway, very poignant. A big component of his character was this terrible insecurity over his impoverished childhood and young manhood, and in particular, his lack of education. He was very aware that he had gone to Southwest Texas State Teachers College, a tiny little school in a very isolated part of the remote Hill Country. Only one member of the faculty had a Ph.D.; several had no degree at all. He himself said, I went to the poor boys' school. If you were in Texas and you had enough money to go to the University of Texas, you went to the University of Texas. If you had almost no money at all, you went to Southwest Texas State Teachers College. He could turn it into a joke. He used to say in his Cabinet meetings, There are eight guys from Harvard here, and one from Southwest Texas. But it wasn't funny to him.

This insecurity was so deep that sometimes it's hard even to write about it without feeling like crying yourself. You know, when he was Majority Leader, he went to a NATO conference in Paris. He had never been to Paris before, and he was reluctant to leave his hotel room because he was afraid he would make a fool of himself. When he had to go to a formal dinner there, he brought his speechwriter, another Texas boy, another poor Texas boy, named Horace Busby, along with him. And Busby recalls how Johnson, sitting near the head of the table, would glare down at him, the length of the table, to make sure that Busby wasn't using the wrong fork and embarrassing him.

And there was another dinner in Paris. Johnson decided, at the last minute, not to go. And Busby, who did go, recalled that a member of the French Senate came up to him and asked where Johnson was, and Busby answered, He couldn't come tonight. And the French senator said, Oh I was so looking forward to meeting the greatest Parliamentarian in the Western world. The greatest Parliamentarian in the Western world. He was afraid to go to the dinner.

Looking at Lyndon Johnson passing the Civil Rights Act of 1964, however, gives us a chance to understand exactly what that French minister meant. Johnson takes up the cause of civil rights four days after John Kennedy's assassination. He tells Congress: "We have talked long enough in this country about equal rights. We have talked for one hundred years or more. It is time now to write the next chapter, and to write it in the books of law."

The books of law. A law. That was what Johnson felt mattered. An executive order, as we're all learning now to our sorrow, is just a piece of paper and can be repealed by another piece of paper. But to write it in the books of law—once you succeed in that, it's not so easy to change. When you look at the newsreels of that speech, you see that the southerners, the committee chairmen: Russell of Armed Services, Byrd of Finance, Ellender of Agriculture, Robertson of Banking, Eastland of Judiciary, Hill of Labor,

Johnston of Civil Service, Jordan of Rules, McClellan of Government Operations—are sitting in front of him, looking up at this man whom they had considered their protégé, who they thought believed the same way. He had convinced them for twenty years that he believed the same way that they did on civil rights.

So I asked the dying Herman Talmadge, How did you feel when you heard that line—"It is time to write it in the books of law?" And again my notes say, "long pause." And then Talmadge said, "Disappointed. Angry. Sick."

WHAT MOMENTS OF DRAMA there are in the passage of the 1964 Civil Rights Act! As you're writing them, you're constantly thinking: are you making them *too* dramatic, more dramatic than they were? More than the facts will support? But the facts are plenty dramatic.

I wrote the scenes when he's inviting the civil rights leaders to the Oval Office. There are five great leaders: there's the oldest, and most venerable and to me the most courageous of all of them, because he had been fighting for civil rights for forty years before this: A. Philip Randolph of the Brotherhood of Sleeping Car Porters. And there were Roy Wilkins of the National Association for the Advancement of Colored People, Whitney Young of the National Urban League, James Farmer of the Congress of Racial Equality, CORE, and of course Martin Luther King, Jr.

So Johnson's secretary, Marie Fehmer, says, Should I bring them in as a group? Well, George Brown once said to me in explaining Lyndon Johnson's genius: Lyndon Johnson was the greatest salesman one-on-one who ever lived. No, Johnson tells Marie, not as a group, schedule them one by one. And he doesn't just talk to each of them. He gives them a focus, not a vague statement of principle, but a specific goal: to pass a discharge petition, a procedural device that the Republicans are opposing ostensibly on procedural grounds but in reality to cover their opposition to civil rights. And he explains to these leaders what has to be done: that without the petition there isn't going to be a vote on the bill. We've got to make people understand somehow that they either sign the petition or they're against civil rights. In this meeting, Johnson is in his rocking chair, Roy Wilkins on one of the sofas in the Oval Office. And Johnson pulls the rocking chair over to Wilkins, knee to knee.

Wilkins had dealt with Lyndon Johnson for years, decades, in fact. And he says in his autobiography that he had felt that "with Johnson, you never quite knew if he was out to lift your heart or your wallet." Wilkins doesn't feel that way anymore. How do we know that? We know because we can hear the tape of another telephone conversation. It's a conversation from December 23, 1963, 10:30 at night. Johnson is still in the Oval Office working. He calls Roy Wilkins, asks him for suggestions about the State of the Union Address, which he has to give in three weeks. He asks Wilkins whom to appoint to a civil rights commission, he says he needs a Mexican-American, we don't have enough Mexican-Americans in positions here, do you know one that we can trust? Wilkins gives him some suggestions. Johnson says good night. But Wilkins doesn't let him hang up. Wilkins says, "Now Mr. President, may I say just a word to you? . . . *Please* take care of yourself." Johnson says, "I'm going to. I'm going to." Wilkins says, "Please take care of yourself. *We need you.*"

The Civil Rights Act of 1964 is not only a story of heroism on the barricades, it's also a study, a case study, of presidential leadership, it's a case study of presidential power, of how a President can be a force for social justice, of how a President can be a creator of social justice.

NOW IT'S 1965. And "We Shall Overcome" is being sung again, and this time it wasn't being sung just in the South or just in churches or in synagogues. This time it was being sung in front of the White House. I wrote about that: You know at that time Pennsylvania Avenue was not closed off as it is now, so the protesters could come and march and sing right up against that black iron fence in front of the White House. And they're singing it in front of the White House in March, 1965, because that was the month of Selma, Alabama, the March on the Edmund Pettus Bridge. I wrote, "If it was a hymn of demand and defiance, the demands the civil rights movement was making could, its leaders felt, ultimately be met only through the power and the leadership of the President, Lyndon Baines Johnson, who, at the same time, was a target of their defiance." Although Johnson had passed the civil rights bill in 1964, it didn't include what they most wanted, it didn't include what they felt was crucial: a strong provision for voting rights. It's four days after a clergyman, the Reverend James Reeb, was clubbed to death. Still no one has been sent to protect the clergymen who had come from all over the country to take Reeb's place and to protect the marchers. And they didn't believe in Lyndon Johnson. They didn't trust him. They remembered the twenty-year record, they heard his southern accent. He had said that now he would address a joint session of Congress, but the expectation was, it wasn't going to be what they wanted. They didn't think that whatever he was going to ask for was going to be much stronger than the 1964 law.

So outside the White House they are singing "We Shall Overcome." And they're chanting. Remember some of the chants?
"Hey, hey, LBJ/How many kids did you kill today?" "LBJ, just
you wait / See what happens in '68." There is an aspect of that
scene which I find poignant. You can't hear what's being shouted
on Pennsylvania Avenue in the Oval Office, but you can hear it
in the mansion, in the family quarters, in the bedrooms, in the
family dining room, where Johnson would be sitting with his wife
and his daughters. You can hear the chants and the songs there.
Just think: How horrible it must be to be sitting there with your
daughters, and they're hearing "Hey, hey, LBJ."

Interviewing: if you talk to people long enough, if you talk to
them enough times, you find out things from them that maybe
they didn't even realize they knew. Take the evening of March 15,
1965. Johnson is going to address a joint session of Congress and
he comes out of the White House and gets into the backseat of
the limousine for his ride to Capitol Hill. Three of his assistants,
Richard Goodwin, Horace Busby, and Jack Valenti, were sitting
on the limousine's jump seats facing him. I never got to talk to
Jack Valenti about that ride, but I talked to Goodwin and Busby,
and I also interviewed George Reedy, who talked to all three of
them the next day, and I asked Reedy what they had told him. I
kept asking Goodwin and Busby, What was the ride like? "What
did you see? What did you *see*?" My interviewees sometimes get
quite annoyed with me because I keep asking them "What did
you see?" "If I was standing beside you at the time, what would
I have seen?" I've had people get really angry at me. But if you
ask it often enough, sometimes you *make* them *see*. So finally

Busby said, Well, you know Lyndon Johnson was really *big*. And sitting on that backseat, the reading light was behind him, so he was mostly in shadow, and somehow that made him seem even bigger. And it made those huge ears of his even bigger. And his face was mostly in shadows. You saw that big nose and that big jutting jaw. I didn't stop. "Come on, Buzz, what did you *see*?" And he finally said, "Well, you know—his *hands*. His hands were huge, big, mottled things. He had the looseleaf notebook with the speech open on his lap, so you saw those big hands turning the pages. And he was concentrating so fiercely. He never looked up on that whole ride. A hand would snatch at the next page while he was reading the one before it. What you saw—what I remember most about that ride—were the hands. And the fierceness of his concentration—that just filled the car." So thanks, Buzz. Now I had more of a feeling of what that ride was like.

And then you also ask—another question that over the years has gotten more people angry at me than I could count—"What did you hear?" And Buzz and Goodwin say, Nothing. He didn't say one word of hello to us when he got into the car, and he didn't say one word the whole ride up there. No one said a word. You would have thought the ride to Capitol Hill was made in complete silence. I remember asking Horace Busby over and over. Oh, Buzz used to get so angry at me. "Listen, Caro, you've asked me that how many times already?" But Buzz was my friend. He was a great friend to have. His name has now been just about completely lost to history, but he was the assistant who for many, many years was closest to Lyndon Johnson. He worked for him ever since he was a student at the University of Texas, and Johnson in many ways regarded him as the son he never had. I had twenty-two separate interviews with Buzz. Formal interviews.

But in addition I used to call him day after day as I was writing to ask him if he remembered some detail I had forgotten to ask about. My typed single-space notes on our interviews are 142 pages. Buzz was one of the smartest analyzers of politics and people I ever met. We became great friends and we used to go out to dinner together. Buzz had quite a crush on Ina. Once he had a stroke, and when he got out of the hospital, he wrote Ina a letter. He wrote that, when he was afraid he was going to die, he thought, "It will be hard on Robert, nobody else can tell him about the vice presidency." The letter was typed; he could still type. But when he tried to sign his name in ink, he could only make a scrawling, shaky "B." Ina cried when she saw that. I may have teared up a little, too. But Buzz recovered, and was a help to me until the end.

When I was asking him about what the three aides heard on the ride to the Capitol, Buzz at first—and second, and third, etc.—replied, Well, nothing. He didn't say anything. So I said something like, So the ride was in complete silence? And then he finally said, "Well, I guess except for when the car passed out through the gates." He meant the gates of the White House onto Pennsylvania Avenue to turn right and go to Capitol Hill. The pickets were there. And Buzz said, Well, they were singing "We Shall Overcome." And they sang it as we came out, "as if," I wrote, "to tell Lyndon Johnson to his face, 'We'll win without you.'" Busby and Goodwin said Johnson never looked up as they passed the pickets. But Busby knew Johnson, and he knew his expressions. So I said to Busby, Well, did he hear them? And Busby said, He heard them.

And of course the speech that Johnson gave is one of the greatest speeches, one of the greatest moments in American history. I watch it over and over. I'm thrilled every time. He said, "Their cause must be our cause too. Because it is not just Negroes, but really it is all of us who must overcome the crippling legacy of bigotry and injustice. And we shall overcome."

There are a number of testimonies to the power of that speech. One is that Martin Luther King was listening to it in the living room of one of his supporters in Selma. His aides were there, and when Johnson spoke that line, they turned to look at Martin Luther King, and he was crying. And that was the only time they ever saw Martin Luther King cry. Another proof of the speech's power I got from Busby and Goodwin: when the limousine was coming back to the White House and turned in to the White House gates, the turn was made in silence. The pickets were gone.

In that year Lyndon Johnson passed Medicaid, Medicare, a slew of education bills, Head Start, the immigration bill, many War on Poverty bills.

So how do you write about the Sixties? You could say that if you were just going up to July, 1965, it was a decade of great strides toward social justice. That it was sort of a decade of hope, and of the song that embodied that hope, "We Shall Overcome."

BUT THAT WAS NOT all the Sixties were. And as I said, that's not the only song that evokes and defines the Sixties. The other song is a very different song, a song not of hope but of despair. It symbolized some other, very different aspects of America. By the time this song was written, in 1967, a lot had changed. Actually, it had been changing all during the time that Lyndon Johnson was passing those bills, because he had managed to keep the country from focusing on the fact that he was preparing to escalate the Vietnam War. All the time that he was passing those bills, the preparations for the escalation were going on. Just about the time he had the last one passed, in July—a Medicare bill on July 30, 1965—he escalated the war.

There were 23,000 American troops in Vietnam when Lyndon Johnson took office. By the end of 1965, there would be 184,000 there. By the end of his presidency, there would be 586,000 there. There were before the war ended 58,000 American dead, and that's the figure you keep hearing when people talk, 58,000 dead. But what of the others? The number of seriously wounded, defined as seriously wounded Americans, was 288,000. Blinded, for instance, amputations, for instance, young men waking up in a hospital and looking down at the place where their legs used to be. Plus the Vietnamese dead. I've been trying for years to get accurate figures on that: the South Vietnamese civilians, South Vietnamese soldiers, North Vietnamese civilians, North Vietnamese soldiers, who died in that war. I don't yet have figures that I regard as reliable, but I'm going to get them. I can say now that the number is more than two million. We dropped more bombs on Vietnam than we dropped on Germany in all of World War II. And we dropped some of them on little villages, where the B-52s that were bombing them flew so high that not only were they invisible, but you couldn't hear them from the ground, so these villages never knew they were being bombed until the bombs actually hit.

There are a lot of songs written about Vietnam, of course. "Where Have All the Flowers Gone?" "Where have all the young men gone, Gone for soldiers every one." But there is, for me, another song: "Waist deep in the Big Muddy / And the big fool says to push on. Waist deep in the Big Muddy, and the big fool says to push on."

I picked that song because I learned, from books, from articles, from interviews, the story behind the song, and to me that story tells quite a bit about America. When it was sung on television for the first time, in 1967, on the hugely popular *Smothers Brothers* show, by Pete Seeger, the fact that Seeger was singing it was notable in itself, because it was the first time that he had been allowed to appear on broadcast television, or on any national radio show either, for seventeen years. Because in 1950, seventeen years earlier, Seeger had refused to name names before the House Un-American Activities Committee, or to tell them whether or not he was then or had ever been a member of the Communist Party, or whom he had voted for in the 1948 election. Because, he said, it was no one's business what party he belonged to, or whom he had voted for. He was, of course, blacklisted, he lost all his bookings, and as I say, he hadn't appeared on TV or national radio for seventeen years. During that time he supported himself by lecturing at colleges, by giving banjo lessons. He and his wife, Toshi, were broke. They bought some very cheap land in the Hudson Valley and with his own hands he built a place for them to live. For years they didn't even have running water or a bathroom.

But sometime in 1967, he remembered, he was watching the nightly newscast, and he saw American troops in Vietnam waist deep and holding their rifles over their heads, trying to wade through the Mekong River. And, Seeger says, It just struck a chord in me, and he wrote this song. "Waist deep in the Big Muddy / And the big fool said to push on. / Waist deep! Neck deep! / And the big fool said to push on." The big fool is a captain, in the song anyway, but a captain was really not who Pete Seeger was talking about. And in the song the captain keeps telling the soldiers to keep coming, and then there's a shot, and a few seconds later, the captain's helmet floated by, and "the Sergeant said, 'Turn around men! / I'm in charge from now.' / And we just made it out of the Big Muddy / With the captain dead and gone." And he sang—"Every time I read the papers / That old feeling comes on; / We're waist deep in the Big Muddy / And the big fool says to push on."

In 1967, Tommy Smothers remembers, "We stuck our heads all the way out and told CBS we wanted to put Pete Seeger on our show." CBS said yes. When they taped the show, Seeger taped four songs. Now it's Sunday night, and the Smothers Brothers are watching it, and there are only three songs. CBS has cut out "Waist Deep in the Big Muddy" because the network felt, as of course was true, that the song was very hostile to Lyndon Johnson. So there's a lot of publicity, a lot of headlines: "CBS Bans Seeger Song for Anti-LBJ Slant." A *lot* of headlines. CBS eventually relents, the show is shown again, this time with the song in.

And of course Pete Seeger goes right on singing about Vietnam with other songs. "Bring 'em home, bring 'em home"—he's singing to Middle America, which keeps saying how much they love their boys in Vietnam. He sings, "If you love our boys in Vietnam / Bring 'em home, bring 'em home."

By 1968, America is a very different place than it was at the start of the Sixties. It's a place of riots, assassinations; it's a decade of assassinations. John Kennedy, Robert Kennedy, Martin Luther King, Malcolm X. Lyndon Johnson doesn't run again in 1968. Four years earlier, he had won by the largest landslide—the largest plurality—in American history. But he doesn't run again. A lot happened during the 1960s to give hope, a lot happened during the 1960s to give despair. They were the years that changed America.

So as I'm writing now: on the one hand there's this absolute fasci nation with how Lyndon Johnson gets these bills passed. Getting some of them passed required his unique political genius. On the other hand, during his presidency, you have a society falling into disorder. Riots in the cities. Fires and riots within a few blocks of the White House. Troops all over Washington.

There is evil and injustice that can be caused by political power, but there is also great good. It seems to me sometimes that people have forgotten this. They've forgotten, for example, what Franklin Roosevelt did: how he transformed people's lives. How he gave hope to people. Now people talk in vague terms about government programs and infrastructure, but they've forgotten the women of the Hill Country and how electricity changed their lives. They've forgotten that when Robert Moses got the Triborough Bridge built in New York, that was infrastructure. To provide enough concrete for its roadways and immense anchorages, cement factories that had been closed by the Depression had to be reopened in a dozen states; to make steel for its girders, fifty separate steel mills had to be fired up. And that one bridge created thousands of jobs: 31,000,000 man hours of work, done in twenty states, went into it. We certainly see how government can work to your detriment today, but people have forgotten what government can do *for* you. They've forgotten the potential of government, the power of government, to transform people's lives for the better.

*

IT TAKES TIME to write all this. The books take time. Truth takes time. Just the research alone, if you add up the time, two months this year, six months the year before, and so on and so forth—Ina and I have spent years of our lives looking through papers at the Johnson Library.

But it's been fascinating trying to figure out how all this happened in America, how political power works, to show the effect of political power on everyone's lives. Whether I knew it or not at the time, I can see now that that's really what I set out to do from the beginning, in my columns at the Princeton paper, my reporting at *Newsday*, and later in my books—to explain how things really work.

The Paris Review Interview

The Art of Biography

Interviewed by James Santel

INTRODUCTION: Since 1976, Robert Caro has devoted himself to *The Years of Lyndon Johnson*, a landmark study of the thirty-sixth president of the United States. The fifth and final volume, now under way, will presumably cover the 1964 election, the passage of the Voting Rights Act and the launch of the Great Society, the deepening of America's involvement in Vietnam, the unrest in the cities and on college campuses, Johnson's decision not to seek reelection, and his retirement and death—enough material, it would seem, for four additional volumes. If there is a question that annoys Caro more than "Do you like Lyndon Johnson?" it is "When will the next book be published?"

This interview took place over the course of four sessions, which were conducted in his Manhattan office, near Columbus Circle. The room is spartan, containing little more than a desk, a sofa, several file cabinets, and large bookcases crammed with well-thumbed volumes on figures like FDR, Al Smith, and the Kennedy brothers—not to mention copies of Caro's own books. One wall is dominated by the large bulletin boards where he pins his outlines, which on several occasions he politely asked me not to read. On the desk sit his Smith-Corona Electra typewriter, a few legal pads, and the room's only ornamental touch: a lamp whose base is a statuette of a charioteer driving two rearing horses.

Caro was born in New York in 1935. He was educated at Horace Mann and Princeton; after college, he worked for a New Jersey newspaper and then *Newsday*. It was there that Caro first heard of Robert Moses, the urban planner who would become the subject of *The Power Broker* (1974), which is not so much a biography as it is a thirteen-hundred-page examination of the political forces that shaped modern-day New York City. After conceiving of the book as a Nieman Fellow at Harvard, Caro persisted through seven difficult years of being, in his words, "plain broke." With the support of his wife, Ina (to make ends meet, she sold their house on Long Island without telling him), he finished, and *The Power Broker* won Caro his first Pulitzer. It also won him the freedom to dedicate himself to his next subject, LBJ. (For his third volume, *Master of the Senate* [2002], he won another Pulitzer.)

In addition to the countless hours he has spent in archives poring over memos and correspondence, Caro has camped out alone in the Texas Hill Country; persuaded former senator Bill Bradley to serve as a model on the Senate floor (Bradley is roughly the same height as Johnson, making him a useful stand-in); and tracked down virtually everyone who ever knew Johnson, from his siblings to his chauffeur. Many of these sources are now deceased, to the frustration of Caro, who valued the ability to call Johnson aides like George Reedy or Horace Busby for spur-of-the-moment clarifications.

Caro now spends most of his days in the Columbus Circle office, writing. Though it is clear that he values uninterrupted time at his desk above almost anything else, he always received me with warm courtesy, except for one occasion, when I arrived fifteen minutes late for our meeting. My tardiness visibly irritated Caro, who had broken off his work in anticipation of my arrival. Waving aside my offer to postpone, he ignored my apologies and began answering my questions in a taut, quiet voice. But as the interview progressed, Caro was warmed by his enthusiasm for his subject, speaking faster and more animatedly, chopping at the air in his eagerness to bring Lyndon Johnson to life.

—*James Santel*

INTERVIEWER: Did you grow up in a house full of books?

CARO: No. My mother got very sick when I was five, and she died when I was eleven. My father was a Polish immigrant. He wasn't really a reader. Books were not part of the house, but my mother, before she died, had my father promise to send me to the Horace Mann School. When I think of my childhood, it's Horace Mann.

I was the editor of the school newspaper. Every Friday, I'd take a trolley up to Yonkers with a rotating cast of the other editors. We'd get off at Getty Square, take all our copy over to a Linotype shop, and then we would stay there while the hot type came out, and when the page was complete they'd ink it and put a piece of paper over it with a roller, and that's how you'd read it.

The nicest thing that's happened to me, really, is that four years ago Horace Mann said they wanted to name a prize after me. I said that would be great, so long as they made it for something that I really wanted to be encouraged. And they said, Well, what is that? I said, I want students to learn that writing, the quality of the prose, matters in non-fiction, that writing matters in history. So they created the Robert Caro Prize for Literary Excellence in the Writing of History. My wife, Ina, is always saying, when I win awards, You're not excited. I say, I'll pretend to be excited if you want. It's like those awards are happening to somebody else, you know? But to go back up there to that school that I loved and to see tacked up on the door of every classroom, DEADLINE FOR THE CARO PRIZE—you say, My God, *that's* exciting.

INTERVIEWER: When you were at Horace Mann, you thought you would pursue journalism?

CARO: Not journalism, necessarily. I wrote short stories for the literary magazine. Then, when I went to Princeton, I wrote for the *Nassau Lit*, the literary magazine, as well as *The Princeton Tiger*. The *Tiger* once devoted almost the whole issue of the magazine to a story I wrote.

But Ina and I wanted to get married right after graduation, so I really needed a job. I got offered a job by *The New York Times*, but they had a rule then that if you had no professional journalism experience—which I didn't—you had to start as a copy boy for, I think, $37.50 a week. We couldn't live on that, and the New Brunswick *Daily Home News* offered me $52 a week. So I went to work for them. But I didn't like working on that paper particularly. The line between the paper and the Democratic county organization was nonexistent, basically. . . . I applied to various newspapers and *Newsday* hired me. I was looking for a crusading-type paper, and that was what *Newsday* was then.

INTERVIEWER: When did you start to gravitate to the kinds of large nonfiction projects that would define your career?

CARO: . . . All the Nieman Fellows had offices then. . . . I sat and thought, How am I going to explain to the readers of *Newsday* about Robert Moses? And the more I thought, the more I realized, My God, I'm never going to be able to do this in the context of daily journalism. To me it seemed that the story of Moses was the story of modern New York. It's going to take a book. . . .

I knew what I really wanted to do for my second book,

because I had come to realize something. I wasn't interested in writing a biography but in writing about political power. I could do urban political power through Robert Moses because he had done something that no one else had done. He had shaped the city with a kind of power we didn't learn about in textbooks, which tell us that, in a democracy, power comes from being elected. He had shaped it with a different kind of power. So if I could find out and explain where he got his power and how he kept it and how he used it, I would be explaining something about the realities of urban power—how raw, naked power really works in cities. And I could do it through his life because I got the right man, the man who did something that no one else had done. I felt it would be great if I could do that kind of book—a book about political power—about national power. And I had had a similar flash about Lyndon Johnson. It was the Senate, it wasn't the presidency. He made the Senate work. For a century before him, the Senate was the same dysfunctional mess it is today. He's Majority Leader for six years, the Senate works, it creates its own bills. He leaves, and the day he leaves it goes back to the way it was. And it's stayed that way until this day. Only he, in the modern era, could make the Senate work. So he, like Moses, had found some new form of political power, and it was national, not urban power. I wanted to do a book about *that*. That's what first drew me to Lyndon Johnson.

Also, I wanted to do Johnson's life in more than one volume because there were things that had been cut out of *The Power Broker* that I regretted having to cut. I cut 350,000 words out of that book. I still miss some of those chapters. I expected to have a fight over this, but before I said anything, Bob Gottlieb said to me, I've been thinking about you and what you ought to do. I know you want to do the La Guardia biography, but I think what you should do is a biography of Lyndon Johnson. And then he said, And I think you should do it in several volumes.

INTERVIEWER: In both books, you took pains over the prose.

CARO: . . . I thought, It matters that people read this. Here was a guy who was never elected to anything, and he had more power than any mayor, more than any governor, more than any mayor or governor combined, and he kept this power for forty-four years, and with it he shaped so much of our lives. I told myself, You have to try to write an introduction that makes the reader feel what you feel about his importance, his fascination as a character, as a human being. I remember rewriting that introduction endless times. For instance, Moses built 627 miles of roads. I said, Come on, that's just a bare statement of fact—how do you make people grasp the immensity of this? And I remembered reading the *Iliad* in college. The *Iliad* did it with lists, you know? With the enumeration of all the nations and all the ships that are sent to Troy to show the magnitude and magnificence of the Trojan War. In college, the professor kept talking about Homer's imagery, Homer's symbolism, et cetera in the *Iliad* and the *Odyssey*. I would be sitting there thinking, Look what Homer does with the *ships*! Not that I would ever think of comparing myself with Homer, but great works of art can be inspiring as models. So in the introduction to *The Power Broker*, I tried listing all the expressways and all the parkways. I hoped that the weight of all the names would give Moses' accomplishment more reality. But then I felt, That's not good enough. Can you put the names into an order that has a rhythm to it that will give them more force and power and, in that way, add to the understanding of the magnitude of the accomplishment? "He built the Major Deegan Expressway, the Van Wyck Expressway, the Sheridan Expressway and the Bruckner Expressway. He built the Gowanus Expressway, the Prospect Expressway, the Whitestone Expressway, the Clearview Expressway and the Throgs Neck Expressway. He built the Cross-Bronx Expressway, the Brooklyn-Queens Expressway, the Nassau Expressway, the Staten Island Expressway and the Long Island Expressway. He built the Harlem River Drive and the West Side Highway." I thought I could have a rhythm that builds, and then change it abruptly in the last sentence. Rhythm matters. Mood matters. Sense of place matters. All these things we talk about with novels, yet I feel that for history and biography to accomplish what they should accomplish, they have to pay as much attention to these devices as novels do.

There's a chapter in *Means of Ascent* called "The Flying Windmill" where Johnson is far behind in his campaign for the Senate. This is his last chance—he's either going to get to the Senate or his career is over. He's desperate, right? Gets out of the hospital and he's far behind in the polls. Someone gives him the idea of flying around Texas in a helicopter. Lyndon Johnson and the helicopter, whipping its side with his Stetson to make it go faster—it's a great dramatic story, and you almost cannot *not* tell the story well because it's such a great story. But I wanted to show desperation. I was trying to write about a desperate man whose last chance is these helicopter trips. I thought, You have the scenes, but it's your job to make the reader feel the desperation. How do you do that? You do it with quotes from his aides showing how desperate he was, how he never slept.

But how else? Rhythm. I tried to infuse the descriptions of his campaigning in that chapter with a rhythm of desperation. And I actually had a note card attached to the lamp on my desk here. I sometimes put a card on there as a reminder to myself. This one said, Is there desperation on this page?

INTERVIEWER: How do you research a subject?

CARO: First you read the books on the subject, then you go to the big newspapers, and all the magazines—*Newsweek, Life, Time, The New York Times, The Washington Post, The Washington Star,* then you go to the newspapers from the little towns. If Johnson made a campaign stop there, you want to see how it's covered in the weekly newspaper.

Then the next thing you do is the documents. There's the Lyndon Johnson papers, but also the papers of everyone else—Roosevelt, Truman, Eisenhower—whom he dealt with. Or for *The Power Broker,* Al Smith's papers, the Herbert Lehman papers, the Harriman papers, the La Guardia papers. . . .

The presidency is different. There's no hope of reading it all. You'd need several lifetimes. But you want to try to do as much as possible, because you never know what you will find. If it's something really important, like a civil rights file, from 1964, 1965, or voting rights, you want to see everything. So I called for everything. But otherwise, you know you're not seeing even a substantial percentage. You hope you're seeing everything that really matters, but you always have this feeling, What's in the rest? . . .

Then come the interviews. You try and find everybody who is alive who dealt with Johnson in any way in this period. Some people you interview over and over. There was this Johnson speechwriter, Horace Busby. I interviewed him twenty-two times. These were the formal interviews. We also had a lot of informal telephone chats. I came to love Buzz. But none of this is enough. You have to ask yourself, Are you making the reader *see* the scene? And that means, Can *you* see the scene? You look at so many books, and it seems like all the writer cares about is getting the facts in. But the facts alone aren't enough.

I'll give you an example. In the first volume, there's a chapter called "The First Campaign." Everyone I talked to about Johnson's first run for Congress would say, I never saw anyone who worked as hard as Lyndon Johnson. Well, it's one thing to tell that to the reader, but how do you show it? Who would really know what this means?

I thought, There's one guy who's with Lyndon Johnson most of the day, and it's not his campaign manager, it's his chauffeur! Because in the Texas Hill Country, a lot of anything is driving—that's 90 percent of the time. His chauffeur was a guy named Carroll Keach. He lived in some place outside Corpus Christi, and it was hard to get to. It was, like, a 180-mile drive or something. But I kept going back to him.

He wasn't a loquacious Texan, he was a laconic Texan. I would ask, What was Johnson doing between campaign stops? And he would say something like, Oh, he was just sitting there in the backseat. I just had to keep asking him questions. I mean, You're driving, Carroll, and Lyndon Johnson is in the backseat? What was he doing in the backseat? Finally, he told me that Johnson often would be talking to himself. So I'd call and say, Carroll, when you said he was talking to himself, what was he saying? Finally, Carroll told me, It was like he was having discussions with himself about whether he had had a successful day, and if he had made a good impression on voters or not. So I'd say, What do you mean by that? How do you know that's what he was talking about?

"Well, lots of the time, he felt he wasn't doing too good. And he would tell himself that it was his own fault."

"What do you mean, he would tell himself it was his own fault?"

"Oh, I don't know, I don't remember."

So I'd call him later and ask again, and I'd finally get something like, Well, Johnson would say to himself, Boy, wasn't that dumb! You know you just lost that ballot box. You lost it, and you need it. And he would talk out—rehearse, over and over, out loud, what he would say to the voters in that precinct the next time.

It was Ed Clark, whom they called the "Secret Boss of Texas," who was one of the first people to say to me, I had never seen anyone work that hard. And finally, after looking at documents like Johnson's daily campaign agenda—which Johnson would put little handwritten notes on—and doing all these interviews, I was able to write, ". . . and Clark didn't know how hard Lyndon Johnson was *really* working. No one knew—with the exception of Carroll Keach. Because only Keach, alone in the car with Johnson for hours each day, knew what Johnson was doing in the car."

That's just one example of the kind of work that can go into making a scene. These things didn't come out in the first or second interview with Carroll Keach but something like the fourth or fifth or tenth. You have to keep going back to important people—people who were important not necessarily because of their status but because of what they saw. For just this chapter, "The First Campaign," I read all the newspapers, the local newspapers, from the little Hill Country towns. And then there were three boxes in the Johnson Library—the records of Johnson's campaign headquarters are boxes one, two, and three of the Johnson House papers. So then Ina and I also looked at, you know, the *Austin American-Statesman*, and Ina drove to all these little towns and found old newspapers like the *Blanco County News* and the *Johnson City Record Courier*. But I interviewed one, two, three, four [*counting names in bibliography*] . . . Well, I got twenty-nine people on that campaign. And I spoke to most of them, like Carroll Keach, many times.

INTERVIEWER: What about your outlining process?

CARO: I can't start writing a book until I've thought it through and can see it whole in my mind. So before I start writing, I boil the book down to three paragraphs, or two, or one—that's when it comes into view. That process might take weeks. And then I turn those paragraphs into an outline of the whole book. That's what you see up here on my wall now—twenty-seven typewritten pages. That's the fifth volume. Then, with the whole book in mind, I go chapter by chapter. I sit down at the typewriter and type an outline of that chapter, let's say if it's a long chapter, seven pages—it's really the chapter in brief, without any of the supporting evidence. Then, each chapter gets a notebook, which I fill with all the materials I want to use—quotations and facts pulled from all of the research I've done.

INTERVIEWER: When you say that the boiling-down process can take weeks, are you doodling? Are you sitting at your desk? What does that process entail?

CARO: The boiling down entails writing those paragraphs over maybe . . . I can't even tell you how many times, over and over and over. The whole time, I'm saying to myself, No, *that's* not exactly what you're trying to do in this book.

If you saw me during this process, in the first place you'd see a guy in a very bad mood. It's very frustrating. I can't actually say anything nice about this part of the work. It's a terrible time for me. I sometimes think, You're never going to get it. There's just so much stuff to put in this book. You're never going to have a unified book with a drive from beginning to end, a single narrative, a single driving theme from beginning to end. There's just too much stuff.

I come home and Ina doesn't even want to see me for the first several hours, because I'm all wound up. I get up during the night to write that couple of paragraphs. I think, Oh, I've got it, I've got it, and then I get up in the morning and I look at it and I say, No, this isn't it. But of course if I finally get the narrative theme, then while I'm writing the book, every time there is a digression—and I have large digressions—I have an easier time bringing the digression back to my theme and keeping the theme in the digression, so the unity, the story, is there in the narrative all the time . . . I hope.

INTERVIEWER: When you say that's not "it," what is "it"?

CARO: Let's say *The Path to Power*. That first volume tries to show what the country was like that Johnson came out of, why he wanted so badly to get out of it, how he got out of it, and how he got his first national power in Washington through the use of money. That's basically the first volume—at the end he loses his first Senate race, but it's pretty clear he's going to come back.

When you distill the book down like that, a lot becomes so much easier. For example, bringing electricity to the Hill Country. In all these early biographies of Johnson, the fact that he founded the largest electricity co-op and brought electricity to the Hill Country gets a few pages, if that—sometimes it only gets a paragraph. But when I was interviewing people out there, they would say, No matter what Lyndon was like, we loved him because he brought the lights. So I suddenly said, God, this bringing the lights is something meaningful. I know what bringing the lights means—it's creating an electricity co-op. But I suddenly saw that he changed this country. This one man changed the lives of more than two hundred thousand people. He brought them into the modern world. Against unbelievable obstacles. That's genius, that's governmental genius. It's terribly significant. So I have to show that significance, make the reader see it—and feel it, too, so the reader can feel like the people of the Hill Country felt. So, you can go off in a direction and show how hard it was to do this—how there was no dam, how the Rural Electrification Administration would never lay all these power lines, and how he overcame that—but you're not losing the single thrust of the book, it's all coming back to how he got out of the Hill Country and what he did for it once he had power.

Getting that boiled-down paragraph or two is terribly hard, but I have to tell you that my experience is that if you get it, the whole next seven years is easier. When you have it, it's so comforting, because you're typing away, and you can look over—it's usually stuck on the wall right there, but I don't want you to see it, actually. I put it away. I don't like anyone to see my notes. But you can look over there and say, You're doing this whole thing on civil rights—let's take *Master of the Senate*—the whole history of the civil rights movement. Is this fitting in with those three paragraphs? How is it fitting in? What you just wrote is good, but it's not fitting in. So you have to throw it away or find a way to make it fit in. So it's very comforting to have that.

INTERVIEWER: Is that your gauge of when the writing is going well—when it's fitting in to that paragraph?

CARO: I'm not sure I ever think the writing is going well. Every day I reread what I wrote the day before, and I've learned from hard experience that it's a real mistake to get too confident about what I've written. I do so much writing and rewriting. And Knopf knows. I rewrite the galleys completely. I even rewrite in page proofs, which they don't actually allow you to do, but they've been very good to me. I'd rewrite in the finished book if I could. . . .

INTERVIEWER: Do you work from nine to five?

CARO: I generally get up around seven or so, and I walk to work through Central Park outlining the first paragraphs that I'm going to write that day. But the thing is, as you get into a chapter, you get wound up. You wake up excited—I don't mean "thrilled" excited but "I want to get in there," so I get up earlier and earlier.

I work pretty long days. If I'm doing research, I can have lunch with friends, but if I'm writing, I have a sandwich at my desk. The guy I order from at the Cosmic Diner, John, he knows my voice.

INTERVIEWER: Do you set daily quotas?

CARO: I have to, because I have a wonderful relationship with my editor and my publisher. I have no real deadlines. I'm never asked, When are you going to deliver? So it's easy to fool yourself that you're really working hard when you're not. And I'm naturally lazy. So what I do is—people laugh at me—I put on a jacket and a tie to come to work, because when I was young, everybody wore jackets and ties to work, and I want to remind myself that I'm going to a job. I have to produce. I write down how many words I've done in a day. Not to the word—I count the lines. I do it as we used to do it in the newspaper business, ten words to a line. I do a lot of little things to try to make me remember it's a job.

I try to do at least three pages a day. Some days you don't, but without some kind of quota, I think you're fooling yourself.

INTERVIEWER: How do you create vivid character studies while staying true to the factual demands of biography?

CARO: You try to learn as much about the people as you can. I try never to give psychohistory. . . . It's as hard to understand someone you're writing about as it is to understand someone in real life, but there are a lot of objective facts about their lives and actions, and the more of them you learn, the closer you come to whatever understanding is possible.

That's especially true when it comes to describing Johnson, whom I met only once, only very briefly. With Johnson, if you went around on my interviews with me, in every interview probably, I'm asking—let's say Joe Califano, one of Johnson's aides—So if I were standing next to you in this scene in the Oval Office, Joe, what would I see? They never understand. They kind of hesitate—they don't know what I mean. And I would say, Was he sitting behind the desk or was he getting up to walk around? And they might say—and this actually happened—Well, he jumped up from that desk all the time because he had the wire tickers over there. He had these three wire tickers, and he'd go over to them every few minutes to look.

So I would ask, But what were you seeing? *How* would he look at the wire tickers?

"Well, you know, it was interesting, it was like he couldn't wait for the next lines to come, so he'd open the lid, and he'd grab the paper with two hands, as if he was trying to pull it out of the machine."

So you keep saying, What would I *see?* Sometimes these people get angry because I'm asking the same question over and over again.

If you just keep doing it, it's amazing what comes out of people. Eventually, a lot of people tell you about his bad breath. And the couches—if he wanted something from you in the Senate cloakroom, Johnson would take you over to sit on the couches. The same with the Oval Office.

So I'd ask, What was it like sitting on those couches? And people would say something like, He'd be towering over you, leaning over you.

So you keep saying, What was it like sitting there?

They'd say, Oh, I remember those couches. They were so downy you thought you'd never get up. And then you realize that Johnson *made* the couches in the Oval Office softer so people would sink down and he, sitting in his rocking chair, would be higher, towering over them.

I spent a large part of these last decades trying to *see* Johnson. It's a product of hundreds and hundreds of interviews. . . .

INTERVIEWER: You seem to describe Johnson in epic terms. Do you consider your biographies epics?

CARO: I don't think about my work in terms like that. It's true that I think of the Johnson books in terms of very large historical events and trends, because the books are the story not just of Lyndon Johnson, although even in those terms it's a monumental story—the desperate young man who pulled himself out of this incredibly lonely and impoverished place, who rose to the very height of power in America, what he had always dreamed of, and then gave it up. But the books are also supposed to be a picture of America during the years of Lyndon Johnson. That's why they're called *The Years of Lyndon Johnson*. I mean, when I was starting *The Power Broker* and when I was starting the first Johnson volume, I said, You don't really have to show what the Depression is like in New York City or what it's like in Texas. That's been done. But I quickly realized that if I was going to do in these books what I wanted to do, I had to do the whole picture of what America was like.

So here is this figure—a huge figure—this young man who's rising, who's ruthless and cruel, nothing can stand in the way of his ambition. And who at the same time has this immense compassion, along with a very rare talent—a genius, really—for transmuting compassion into something concrete, into legislative achievement. That's why, of all the sentences Johnson spoke in his speeches, I think one of the most meaningful was when he was speaking about John Kennedy's civil rights program, he said, "It is time now to write it in the books of law." Lyndon Johnson, if I do him right, he's this huge figure with these complexities. I'm trying to show him moving through American history, rising through it, political step by political step. And what was America in his times? And how did he change America? Because certainly he changed America. But you're not *making* it a monumental story on a grand scale. It *is* a monumental story on a grand scale.

Take this book I'm writing now. You see Johnson when finally he has the power to change America, and America is a completely different place when he leaves the presidency in January, 1969 than it is when he becomes president, on the day John Kennedy is assassinated. So what is this? Great, huge protagonists—I don't want to use the word *heroes*—fighting great battles. Think of the battles. Congress's mighty, invincible Southern Caucus and the battle for civil rights. The mighty robber barons and Robert Moses' battle for the parkways. You say to yourself, I've got to write in a way that makes people realize that this isn't just politics.

When Moses has this great dream of the parkways, how do I show the greatness of the dream? How do I show the magnitude of the fight? I have to show the immense power of the men he defeated. That means showing the whole background of the robber barons. You've got to make people see the robber barons, with these magnificent estates in the path of the parkways he wanted to build so poor families from the city could get to the Long Island beaches. You can't just say, The robber barons were opposed to him.

And again, you have to base all of this in fact. When Moses was walking around Long Island looking at the mansions of the robber barons, he once had a companion walking with him. I found the man who walked with him. So I could really describe those walks and those great estates. This is the man who's going to take on the entrenched power of the Gilded Age and the robber barons and he's going to beat them. So I wrote,

And in the summer of 1923, Moses went back to tramping around Long Island. "I went with him once," a friend says. "We walked all day through one piece of beautiful wild country after another. And he never slowed down. He was tireless." ... He walked alone through vast, empty shuttered mansions, through potato fields where farmers worked peacefully, not knowing that the man looking at them was planning to take their fields away. Walls and guards kept him from getting a good look from paved public roads at the route he was considering for the northern parkway, but he discovered unpaved back roads through many of the estates, and he spent days walking along those deserted paths, a solitary figure with a long stride. Through the trees he could see the great castles; at their gates, on little black and gold signs, he could see the names of the great barons who had built them. And the barons, private behind their walls, did not know that staring at those walls was a man determined to tear them down.

This is a battle that no one knows. And my books are full of these battles. You think of Robert Moses striking down a score of foes, of Lyndon Johnson defeating the southern senators, and you say, These were heroic, majestic battles of American history. If I want to be true to what I'm trying to do, I have to try to make readers see the grandeur and the majesty. I have to make the readers see the epic, the almost insurmountable difficulties confronting the man trying to pass the Civil Rights Act of 1957, when the Senate is almost completely controlled by the South.

If you want to be true to these people—these very rare figures who accomplished monumental, world-changing feats—you have to picture the things they're doing on a monumental, world-changing scale. Really, my books are an examination of what power does to people. Power doesn't always corrupt, and you can see it in the case of, for example, Al Smith or Sam Rayburn. There, power cleanses. But what power *always* does is reveal, because when you're climbing, you have to conceal from people what it is you're really willing to do, what it is you want to do. But once you get enough power, once you're there, where you wanted to be all along, then you can see what the protagonist wanted to do all along, because now he's doing it. With Robert Moses, you see power becoming an end in itself, transforming him into an utterly ruthless person. In *The Passage of Power*, I describe the speechwriter Dick Goodwin trying to find out if Johnson is sincere about civil rights, and Johnson tells him, I swore to myself when I was teaching those kids in Cotulla that if I ever had the power, I was going to help them. Now I have the power and I mean to use it. You see what Johnson wanted to do all along. Or at least *a* thing he wanted to do all along . . .

Somewhere in *The Power Broker* I write that regard for power means disregard of those without power. I mean, we're really talking about justice and injustice. . . . I remember being filled with real anger at the injustice of what Moses did to the people of East Tremont. I thought, God, look what Moses did here. This was political power. You have to write not only about the man who wields the sword, but also about the people on whom it is wielded.

It's even more complicated with Johnson. Domestically, he did such magnificent things as president. Everyone wants to say that if it weren't for Vietnam, he would've been one of the greatest presidents. But "if it weren't for Vietnam" is not an adequate phrase. You have to give equal weight to both the domestic and Vietnam. Medicare. The Voting Rights Act. The Civil Rights Act. Head Start. So many different education bills. You're filled with admiration for his genius, over and over again. Watching some legislative maneuver, you're saying, Wow, how did he do that, I didn't know you could do that! And then in the same book, you have Vietnam. This last volume is a very complex book to write.

INTERVIEWER: There seems to be a real idealism behind your project—you hope the books serve a larger civic purpose.

CARO: Well, you always hope something. I think the more light that can be thrown on the actual processes we're voting about, the better. We live in a democracy, so ultimately, even despite a Robert Moses, a lot of political power comes from our votes. The more we understand about the realities of the political process, the better informed our votes will be. And then, presumably, in some very diffuse, very inchoate way, the better our country will be.

The Paris Review, Spring 2016

A NOTE ON THE TYPE

This book was set in Janson, a typeface named for the Dutchman
Anton Janson, but is actually the work of Nicholas Kis (1650–
1702). The type is an excellent example of the influential and
sturdy Dutch types that prevailed in England up to the time
William Caslon (1692–1766) developed his own incomparable
designs from them.

Composed by North Market Street Graphics,
Lancaster, Pennsylvania

Printed and bound by Berryville Graphics,
Berryville, Virginia

Designed by Cassandra J. Pappas

Herman Brown -- Brown & Root had been given the contract to construct
the PEC lines -- was able
to hire men who were known to be very hard workers.

The poles that would carry the electrical lines had

They needed to be. ~~to be sunk in rock.~~ Brown & Root's mechanical hole-diggers *broke on the*
hard Hill Country rock ~~was too~~ Every hole had to be

dug mostly by hand. Eight or ten-man crews would pile onto flat-bed

trucks -- which also carried their lunch and water -- in the morning
Some trucks carried axe-mens to hack paths through the cedar The next contained
and head out into the hills. Every three or four hundred feet, two
the hole-diggers "the hole-diggers" digging a ~~hole~~ by pounding the
~~men~~ would drop off and begin

ends of crowbars into the limestone. After the hole reached a depth of six inches,

half a stick of dynamite was exploded in it, to loosen the

rock below, but that, too, had to be dug out by hand.

"Swinging crowbars up and down -- that's hard labor," Babe

Smith says. "That's back-breaking labor." But the hole-diggers

had incentive. For after
and "pikemen"
the hole-digging teams came the the pole-setters who, in teams
poles *pine from East Texas*
of three, set the thirty-five foot poles into the rock
(lifting them with sharp-pointed pikes) and then
attached
the "framers" who set the insulators and then *the "stringers"* who strung

the wires, and at the end of the day the hole-diggers
could see the result of their work stretching out behind them — poles
towering above the cedar, silvery lines against the sapphire sky and the homes the wires were

"these workers — they were the men of
heading toward were their own homes. ~~As soldiers fight hardest when~~
the co-operative," Smith says. Gratitude was a spur also, after the crews
~~fighting for the homes of their families, the hole-diggers of the~~
didn't have to eat the cold lunch they had brought. A woman would see a
~~crew toiling toward her home, "imagine the lights" And~~
~~the very best food that the family could afford~~
~~hundred poles a day considered impossible in such rock.~~